THE ROLE OF INTERUNIVERSITY ATHLETICS:
A CANADIAN PERSPECTIVE

EDITED by
A.W. TAYLOR, PhD.

**PROCEEDINGS OF A
CONFERENCE SPONSORED
BY THE
CANADIAN COUNCIL OF
UNIVERSITY PHYSICAL
EDUCATION
ADMINISTRATORS**

Canadian Cataloguing in Publication Data

Taylor, Albert W.
    The role of interuniversity athletics

ISBN 0-9691619-6-4

1. College sports - Canada.   I. Title.

GV351.5.C3T38 1986   769'.07'1171   C86-094480-8

Copyright© 1986 by **Sports Dynamics**

Printed in Canada by Pear Creative Ltd., 534 Adelaide St., London, Ontario (519) 434-4744

TABLE OF CONTENTS

INVITED SPEAKERS

CHARD, E.A.	Registrar, Saint Mary's University
CONNELL, G.E.	President, University of Toronto
DEWAR, J.	Past Dean, School of Physical Education University of Saskatchewan
HOFFMAN, A.	Director, Sport Canada
JACKSON, R.	President, Canadian Olympic Association
JANZEN, H.	Dean, Faculty of Physical Education and Recreation Studies, The University of Manitoba
KEYES, M.	Director, School of Physical Education and Athletics McMaster University
MACINTOSH, D.	Acting Director, School of Physical and Health Education, Queen's University
MACKINNON, G.A.	President, St. Francix Xavier University
MOHR, L.E.	M.B.A. Student and Athlete, Queen's University
OUELLET, J-G	Vice Recteur, Universite de Sherbrooke
PEDERSON, K.G.	President, The University of Western Ontario
POMFRET, M.	President, Canada West University Athletic Association
SEMOTIUK, D.M.	Chairman, Intercollegiate Athletics Program, The University of Western Ontario
TAYLOR, A.W.	President, Canadian Council of University Physical Education Administrators

PARTICIPANTS

NAME	TITLE	UNIVERSITY
Dr. J. R. C. Perkin	President	Acadia
Dr. G. Wright	Director, School of Physical Education	Acadia
Dr. M. Smith	Assistant Dean, Faculty of Physical Education	Alberta
Dr. R. Steadward	Chairman, Department of Athletics	Alberta
Dr. C. I. H. Nicholl	Principal	Bishops
Dr. R. Hindmarch	Chairman, Intercollegiate Athletics	British Columbia
Dr. R. Morford	Director, School of Physical Education and Recreation	British Columbia
Mrs. M. Pomfret	President, Canada West Athletic Association	British Columbia
Dr. J. R. Mallea	President	Brandon
Dr. A. Lowenberger	Director, School of Physical Education	Brock
Dr. W. E. Bejekel	President	Carleton
Ms. G. Blake	Coordinator of Women's Athletics	Carleton
Mr. K. Harris	Director of Athletics	Carleton
Dr. E. Enos	Director of Athletics	Concordia
Prof. G. Martin	Vice Rector Services	Concordia
Mr. W. MacDonald	Coordinator of Intercollegiate Athletics	Dalhousie
Dr. L. Maloney	Director, School of Recreation, Physical and Health Education	Dalhousie
Mr. David Copp	Director of Athletics	Guelph
Mr. Paul Gilmor	Provost	Guelph
Ms. Sandy Knox	Director of Athletics	Laurentian
Mr. K. Coffin	Director of Athletics	Lakehead
Dr. R. Lappage	Acting Director, School of Physical Education and Health	Lakehead
Dr. J. Whitfield	Vice-President	Lakehead
Mrs. J. Fromson	Director of Athletics	Manitoba
Dr. H. Janzen	Dean, School of Physical Education	Manitoba
Mr. J. Snidal	-	Manitoba

Mr. Robert Dubeau	Director of Athletics	McGill
Dr. Mary Keyes	Director, School of Physical Education and Athletics	McMaster
Mr. F. Butler	Coordinator of Varsity Athletics	Memorial
Dr. L. Harris	President	Memorial
Dr. F. Mills	Chairman, Board of Governors	Mt. Allison
Mr. J. Born	Director of Athletics	New Brunswick
Dr. W. MacGillivary	Dean, Faculty of Physical Education & Recreation	New Brunswick
Dr. C. W. J. Eliot	President	Prince Edward Island
Mr. R. Carnegie	Director of Athletics	Queen's
Mr. L. Mohr	Graduate Student & Speaker	Queen's
Dr. D. MacIntosh	Acting Director, School of Physical and Health Education	Queen's
Mr. R. Powers	Chairman, University Council on Student Affairs and Rector	Queen's
Ms. A. Turnball	Coordinator of Women's Intercollegiate Athletics	Queen's
Dr. L. Barber	President	Regina
Dr. N. Sherlock	Dean, Faculty of Physical Activity Studies	Regina
Mr. D. White	Coordinator of Athletics	Regina
		Royal Military College
Mr. R. Fullerton	Director of Athletics	Ryerson Polytechnic
Fr. G. A. McKinnon	President	St. Francis Xavier
Dr. B. Mutimer	Director of Physical Education	St. Francis Xavier
Ms. E. Chard	Registrar	Saint Mary's
Dr. K. L. Ozmon	President	Saint Mary's
Dr. J. Dewar	Past Dean, College of Physical Education	Saskatchewan
Dr. R. Mirwald	Dean, College of Physical Education	Saskatchewan
Mr. D. Mounsey	-	Saskatchewan Indian Foundation College
Mr. W. Devries	Executive Director, Administrative Services	Simon Fraser

Dr. J. Dickinson	Director, School of Kinesiology	Simon Fraser
Dr. J. G. Ouellet	Vice-Recteur	Sherbrooke
Mr. G. Chapman	Director of Athletics	Toronto
Dr. G. Connell	President	Toronto
Dr. Y. Daniel	Acting Director, School of Physical Education	Toronto
Mr. P. Wilson	Director of Athletics	Trent
Mr. E. S. Lucy	Director, Employee and Student Services	Waterloo
Dr. A. K. Barney	Professor, Physical Education	Western Ontario
Mr. J. Bone	Athletics Information Officer	Western Ontario
Dr. B. Brown	Professor, Physical Education	Western Ontario
Dr. A. V. Carron	Professor, Physical Education	Western Ontario
Dr. P. Chelladurai	Professor, Physical Education	Western Ontario
Mr. D. Decker	Professor, Physical Education	Western Ontario
Dr. W. Dunn	Past Dean, Dentistry	Western Ontario
Mr. G. Gonser	Professor, Physical Education	Western Ontario
Mr. T. Haggerty	Professor, Physical Education	Western Ontario
Mr. L. Haylor	Professor, Physical Education	Western Ontario
Mr. B. Larose	Professor, Physical Education	Western Ontario
Dr. C. Leith	Provost and Vice-President Academic	Western Ontario
Mrs. H. Luckman	Vice Chairman, Athletics	Western Ontario
Dr. G. Pedersen	President	Western Ontario
Dr. D. Semotiuk	Chairman, Intercollegiate Athletics Program	Western Ontario
Dr. E. Zeigler	Professor, Physical Education	Western Ontario
Mr. R. Boucher	Director of Men's Athletics	Windsor
Ms. M. Prpich	Director of Women's Athletics	Windsor
Dr. M. Salter	Acting Dean, Faculty of Human Kinetics	Windsor
Dr. G. Wood	Vice-President Academic	Windsor
Ms. P. Murray	Coordinator of Women's Athletics	York
Dr. S. Robbins	Chairman and Director, Department of Physical Education and Athletics	York
Prof. T. Meininger	Provost	York
Ms. A. Hoffman	Director	Sport Canada
Dr. S. Neill	Chief, Policy, Planning and Evaluation	Sport Canada
Dr. R. Jackson	President	Canadian Olympic Association
Mr. R. Pugh	Executive Vice-President	CIAU

Dr. A. W. Taylor	President	CCUPEA
P. Y. Boucher	Associate Executive Director and Legal Council	AUCC
Mr. Blanchard		Unknown

OPENING REMARKS

PRESIDENT K.G. PEDERSEN

It is both a pleasure and an honour for me to welcome you to this conference entitled "Conference on Interuniversity Athletics: A Canadian Perspective". I do so both personally and on behalf of The University of Western Ontario.

To all of us who are associated with universities, the education which our students receive takes a great variety of forms. Certainly university education is not restricted to what goes on in the classroom or the library or the computer laboratory. It extends much further and includes a wide variety of social, cultural and physical activities. It is within this latter arena that inter-university athletics plays an important role.

The interface between the primary mission of the university, involving teaching and research activities, and competitive athletics has been one involving much in the way of serious debate. Should there be competitive inter-school competition? How extensive should such programs be? Who should provide the coaching support? Are any forms of athletic scholarship acceptable? These are but a few of the questions that arise. Today's session, involving chief executive officers of our universities along with those directly responsible for administering athletics, should be helpful in our efforts to better define the issues and bring them to more reasoned resolution.

In conclusion, I do want to acknowledge the contributions of The Canadian Council of University Physical Education Administrators (CCUPEA), the Association of Universities and Colleges of Canada (AUCC), and the Canadian Association of University Athletic Directors (CAUAD) all of whom made today possible. My very best wishes for a most successful day.

NEIL B. SHERLOCK

The Canadian Council of University Physical Education Administrators (CCUPEA) was pleased to host, "Interuniversity Athletics: A Canadian Perspective", a conference held at the University of Western Ontario, March 7, 1986.

Invited participants at the Conference included representatives from the: Association of Universities and Colleges of Canada (AUCC); Canadian Association of University Athletic Directors (CAUAD); Canadian Interuniversity Athletic Union (CIAU); Government of Ontario; Sport Canada; and Media.

The Conference was made possible in part through the generosity and support of the CCUPEA, Government of Ontario, Sport Canada, and the University of Western Ontario. We are indebted to these agencies for their contribution and assistance.

Instigation for this conference resulted from growing concerns both philosophical and financial confronting the C.I.A.U. and its member institutions. As one might expect, in a country as vast as Canada, the C.I.A.U., as a national organization, has been unable to adequately rationalize disparate regional and institutional motives and attitudes underlying university athletic programming in Canada.

The conference was designed to encourage discussion and communication between universities and the participating agencies on current issues including:

1. questions of the role or purpose of interuniversity athletics;

2. questions of organizational and structural models for the administration of athletics within institutions;

3. questions of, "Who should pay?", - financing and fund raising for athletics; and,

4. questions of government involvement and commitment to interuniversity athletics including issues surrounding a) "a federal versus provincial jurisdiction?", (b) the threat of reduction or elimination of the Sport Canada Travel Equalization subsidy to university athletics, and c) the impact of Sport Canada's emphasis on elite athlete training centres on the integrity of the CIAU and its Conferences.

Further impetus for the Conference came from the Report of the Special Committee on Intercollegiate Athletics, Council of Ontario Universities, April 30, 1985.

It was further noted that the Atlantic provinces of Canada are conducting a similar study initiated at the presidential level of the institutions.

A final factor leading to the initiation of this conference arose from the realization that the chief sponsors and/or authoritative bodies for interuniversity athletic programming in Canada, namely AUCC, CIAU, CCUPEA, and Sport Canada, had never been caused to meet in common forum.

The CCUPEA in recognizing the disparities, problems, and conflicts between participating institutions and agencies in interuniversity athletics embraced the need and potential value of a forum for review and debate of athletic issues. It should be noted that the purpose and expected outcome of the conference was not necessarily to resolve the issues. This would be a naive and unrealistic expectation. Rather, it was assumed that all parties and participants would benefit from the exchange and interaction resulting from presentations and ensuing discussions. It was anticipated that the conference would provide the participants with a better understanding and appreciation of the diversity of regional and institutional needs and impera- tives in interuniversity athletic programming across Canada. It was our wish that this new found appreciation of differences might foster greater resolve within the CIAU to build structures and conveniences which better accommodate institutional needs across the country.

Obviously if there is to be any true impact from this event it will only come through further review at the regional conference and institutional levels. The CCUPEA lays the challenge of following up, what proved to be a successful athletic debate, before each University institution. The issues discussed at this national conference are even more imperative at the regional and institutional levels if university athletics are to grow in desirable directions.

Finally, the CCUPEA would like to thank all those who participated in "Interuniversity Athletics: a Canadian Perspective". We extend a special thank you to those who set the tone for a successful conference through their presentations and panel participations. To those in attendance at the Confer- ence or who may have cause to review the published proceedings, we wish to acknowledge that the presentations and performances reflected the views of the presenters themselves and not necessarily the CCUPEA. We were confident that this approach would best elicit a reflection of the differences inherent in the fabric of Canadian interuniversity athletics.

The CCUPEA wishes to continue to provide strong advocacy for sound interuniversity athletic programming in Canada. It is our hope that this conference served that purpose.

SECTION 1. INTRODUCTION AND HISTORICAL DEVELOPMENTS

- INTERCOLLEGIATE ATHLETICS IN CANADIAN UNIVERSITIES:
  AN HISTORICAL PERSPECTIVE -- D. MACINTOSH

- A BRIEF LOOK AT EXISTING ATHLETIC PROGRAM DELIVERY
  MODELS IN CANADA -- J. DEWAR

INTERCOLLEGIATE ATHLETICS IN CANADIAN UNIVERSITIES:
AN HISTORICAL PERSPECTIVE

DONALD MACINTOSH

Introduction

The recommendations from the two national studies of intercollegiate athletics which have been undertaken in Canada in recent years serve to set a historical perspective for this conference (Matthews, 1974; AUCC, 1969). The first set of these, (sponsored by the AUCC) came from a larger conference on physical education, sport, and recreation in Canadian universities, held in Toronto in 1966, and with financial assistance from the Fitness and Amateur Sport Directorate. The recommendations regarding intercollegiate athletics suggest much simpler and less rationalized times, and illustrate that many of the issues raised then are still with us. The major recommendations were: first, that intercollegiate athletics should be established as one department in a wider division of physical education and that a female faculty member be responsible for the women's programs; second, that the director of intercollegiate athletics should have "complete decision making authority" but should be advised by a student/faculty athletics committee; third, that the university should take full responsibility for financing all athletics programs and there should be no separate identifiable student athletic fee; fourth, that intercollegiate teams should be coached by full-time faculty members; and, fifth, that financial aid based solely on athletic abilities should be considered an undesirable practice.

The Matthews Report, the second review of intercollegiate athletics, was a more formalized study of athletics and included a cross-country survey of current practices and views on desired standards. It was undertaken in 1973-74 by CIAU/CWIAA and the AUCC, and was supported by a grant from Sport Canada. Intercollegiate athletics had expanded and national championships had become an important issue. As a result, different policies and practices among the various regional conferences became a concern. In particular, athletic scholarships and the recruitment of athletes from the United States were causing conflict and dissention among member institutions. On three major issues, recommendations from the resulting Matthews Report paralleled those from the Toronto conference: first, that universities should, wherever possible, integrate athletics and physical education departments; second, that athletics programs should be financed by the university; and, thirdly, that athletic divisions should be staffed when possible by personnel having qualifications for academic programs. The report, however, recognized that there was growing problems with financing travel in Canadian intercollegiate sport. Consequently it suggested that outside sources be sought for funds for a central travel pool.

The Matthews Report took a strong stand on athletic scholarships, stating that athletic abilities should not be one of the criteria for university loans, bursaries, or scholarships. However, it did raise the possibility of searching for outside financial assistance for athletes. This was the beginning of third party scholarships, i.e., awards to athletes from governments and other groups at arms-length from the university. To resolve the problems associated with recruiting, the Matthews Report recommended that such practices should not take place beyond the bounds of the normal geographical recruiting area for students-at-large. It also recognized the growing problems associated with the dominance in certain sports by athletes from the United States and recommended that standards be established for "Canadian content" in these sports. The Report also recognized the problem of variations of competitive levels among Canadian universities and suggested that tiering of teams in certain major sports should be considered.

The Matthews Report in many ways was nostalgic in nature, and carried with it the implication that if universities clung to traditional values and standards, all would be well in intercollegiate sports. This, of course, was not to be the case. Intercollegiate sport grew in size, importance, and complexity and the recommendations of the Matthews Report proved inadequate for dealing with these new complexities.

Recent Forces

A number of social and economic forces have had a strong impact on Canadian intercollegiate athletics since the tabling of the Matthews report in 1973. Sport, which grew in importance through the 1960s, became a major social force in the 1970s. Sport's affinity for television brought it into the living rooms of millions of Canadians, who hitherto had little or no interest in or knowledge of sport. This made it attractive as a vehicle to sell goods and services. As such, sport became a prime televisions commodity. At the same time, sport became increasingly rationalized. The criteria for evaluating it focused more and more on performance and record; values of contest, versatility, and the combination of a sports career with other avocations, (i.e., the old concept of amateurism,) were pushed to the background.

As sport became an integral part of popular culture, it attracted the interest of government. In the late 1960s, the Federal Liberal Government set out to use sport as an instrument to promote national unity. Success in international sports events was essential to this promotion; thus, the production of high-performance athletes became a major priority of the Ministry of State for Fitness and Amateur Sport. Sport Canada looked upon the universities as the primary source of facilities and expertise for these efforts.

A third factor which has affected intercollegiate athletics in the past decade is the growing financial restraint under which universities are operating. This has been particularly critical for intercollegiate athletics departments because they were under increasing pressure to provide both broader and more intense programs. As a result, athletic departments were forced to look outside the university for financial support.

Critical Issues

These three pressures on intercollegiate sport - the growing importance of sport in society, the increasing desire of government to use Canadian universities to develop high-performance athletes, and the financial constraints placed on universities - have made many of the recommendations in the Matthews Report obsolete. First, the axiom that intercollegiate athletics should be financed entirely from university funds has gone by the boards. This leakage occurred first at the national level, where the CIAU sought sponsors and government funds for national championships. It then spread to the regional level, where sponsors and financial assistance were solicited to support regional competitions and playoffs. Finally, individual universities were forced to find outside funds to supplement internal monies.

This trend has led to a number of problems. First, it has placed pressure on athletic administrators and coaches to become fund-raisers, and as such, has further fragmented their workload and increased their job frustration. Second, it has brought the universities into conflict over the issue of associating intercollegiate athletics with alcohol and tobacco companies because, these groups have been the most eager sponsors. Third, it has raised questions about the extent to which outside sponsors should influence the program itself. The question of who should finance intercollegiate sport, then, is one of the critical issues of the day.

The financial crisis in intercollegiate sport also has brought pressure on those universities that have attempted to maintain a broad-base program, while at the same time to upgrade high profile sports. Some institutions have increased this pressure by narrowing the breadth of their program to concentrate more effectively on certain high profile sports. Can universities continue to serve both masters -- the broad-based program on the one hand and high-performance sport on the other? Can compromise be reached on this issue or is it time to agree to part ways -- some institutions choosing high-performance and others, the broad base?

Increasingly stringent tenure and promotion regulations and policies and the greatly increased demands of high-performance sport on intercollegiate coaches have meant that having coaches as full-time faculty members has become an out-moded standard. In addition, the great increase in the number of intercollegiate sports in many Canadian universities in the 1970s has meant that it was impossible to have the entire sports roster coached by a full-time member of the academic staff. Thus, the trend has been towards hiring coaches on non-academic routes. In turn this has created problems of standards, values, tenure, and secondary employment roles in the university. What are the implications of this trend for intercollegiate sport?

These changes call into question the organizational structure which supports athletics. With a greater concentration on excellence and the need to put intercollegiate athletics on more of a "paying" basis, the gap between athletic departments and academic physical education divisions has widened, even in so-called integrated divisions. The fact that fewer full-time physical education faculty members are now coaching intercollegiate teams has exacerbated this situation. One perceived advantage of integration is that physical education faculty provide a sound educational philosophical base for intercollegiate sport. Given these complexities, what is the best organization structure for intercollegiate sport?

The increasing pressure by government to use university programs as a site for developing high-performance athletes also has raised a number of issues. First, the concentration of these athletes at certain institutions has often created substantial imbalances in competitive level, and in some cases, has resulted in a decrease in the number of competing universities. Second, the time, personnel, facilities, and financial resources needed to support high-performance athletes has meant fewer resources for other aspects of university sport programs. It also has called into question the use of university resources and student athletic fees to support the development of Canada's elite athletes. A concentration on high-performance sport distances the program from the average student and increases the risk of having the program rejected by the general student and faculty body. What then is the role of universities in high-performance sport? Should Canada's high-performance athletes actually compete in university programs, or should they simply train at universities, using the available facilities and expertise?

Another issue which plagues intercollegiate sport is equality of opportunity for women. At a time when it is more widely recognized that women should have equal opportunities and that equal resources should be devoted to women's sport, the universities are faced with shrinking resources. When financial assistance is sought outside the university, women's sport is not as attractive a vehicle for television broadcasts and selling goods as is the case for men. This puts the goal of equality for females in intercollegiate sport in even greater jeopardy. The dominance of males in the membership and decision-making process of the CIAU is another obstacle to resolving this equality issue.

Conclusion

We will not resolve these issues today. Most of them are persistent problems which individual institutions, regional associations, and the CIAU have been grappling with for the last decade. The purpose of this conference is to lay bare these issues so that they are better understood by senior academic administrators, and to set the groundwork for working towards their solution. However, they cannot be resolved without establishing the ground rules. There are different answers to these issues depending upon the purposes of intercollegiate athletics. It will no longer suffice to make do with vague platitudes about these purposes. Such statements in the past served only to provide a broad framework within which each university could apply its own interpretation. Statements of purpose of intercollegiate sport need to be set in concrete terms and related to the critical issues dealt with at this conference. Only in this way can we identify crucial areas of differences of intent, and seek to find compromise solutions within this more realistic framework.

References

AUCC. (1966) Physical Education and Athletics in Canadian Universities and Colleges. Ottawa: Canadian Association of Health, Physical Education, and Recreation.

Matthews, A.W. (1974) Athletics in Canadian Universities. Ottawa: The Association of Universities and Colleges in Canada.

A BRIEF LOOK AT EXISTING ATHLETIC PROGRAM
DELIVERY MODELS IN CANADA

J. DEWAR

Blessed is the man who by strength of hand and swiftness of foot, takes by skill and daring the highest of prizes.
- from Olympian Ode
Pindar, 4th century B.C.

The great competitions in archaic cultures had always formed part of the sacred festivals and were indispensable as health- and happiness-bringing activities. This ritual tie has now been completely severed; sport has become profane, "unholy" in every way and has no organic connection whatever with the structure of society . . . . The ability of modern social techniques to stage mass demonstrations with the maximum of outward show in the field of athletics does not alter the fact that neither the Olympiads nor the organized sports of American Universities nor the loudly trumpeted international contests have, in the smallest degree, raised sport to the level of a culture-creating activity. However important it may be for the players or spectators, it remains sterile. The old play-factor has undergone almost complete atrophy . . .

- from Homo Ludens (1939), by Johan Huizinga

The 'show biz' atmosphere of this new dominant form of sport ("State" sport) has trivialized the traditional value of sport which held forth in Canada until recently. Comparisons with other performers outweigh intrinsic values of self expression, self-actualization, feelings of well-being, and the joy and spontaneity of contact.
- Macintosh, 1986

The Matthews report strove, in 1974, to recommend means whereby the intrinsic educational values of sport would be promoted within Canadian university athletics. The recommendation and structure recommended were to direct the thinking of institutions to models that would lead back from Huzinga's pessimistic perceptions to those of Pindar. As Macintosh (1986) has indicated, the athletic flow of the 70's and 80's has not always been towards blessedness.

The stated objectives of individual university programs and of the CIAU, as an associate of AUCC, were in the years following the report directed to the promotion of these intrinsic values. The improvement in the quality of life of the participant became and continues to be the objective of the programs. Matthews (1974) commented on the future direction as follows:

Now the supply and demand of highly trained people are more in balance (as compared to the period following World War II) and the universities have been able to re-establish their fundamental role: to help people become mores useful to society in a very broad sense and adjust to the very competitive world in which they now live. Viewed in this latter perspective the studies (from a broad cross section of Canadian universities) appear to have arrived at a consensus that athletics, together with physical education, should be regarded as an integral part of the educational process. (p. 15)

Models 1973/1986

The athletic administrative models being used in Canadian universities to implement the programs were categorized and enumerated by the report (1974, p. 15), as found in Table 1.

TABLE 1. RELATIONSHIP OF INTERCOLLEGIATE PROGRAMS TO PHYSICAL EDUCATION PROGRAMS BY NUMBER OF UNIVERSITIES, 1973

	Including Phys. Ed. Degree	Not. Incl. Phys. Ed. Degree	All Programs
Intercollegiate program organized as:			
function of physical education department with same person as director of physical education and athletics	5	5	10
function of physical education department with director of athletics responsible to the director of physical education	14*	2	16
autonomous athletic department with co-ordinated relationship with physical education	10	3	13
autonomous department with no relationship to physical education	4	2	6
athletic department only (no physical education department exists)	–	11	11
Total number of universities	33	23	56

* Included two universities in which physical education program is a major in the faculty of education.

The report recommended that, "physical education and athletic programs . . . into a single administrative unit".

The following model was used to illustrate this structure:

Figure 1

Coordinating Council

Program Chairman

Athletics Coordinator	Physical Education Coordinator

Recreation Committee Phys. Ed. Committee	Intramural Committee Committee	Intercol- legiate Athletics Committee	Instructional Service Ed. Committee	Undergrad. Phys. Degree	Graduate Phys. Degree	Ed.

(only in universities with degree programs)

Another central recommendation dealt with funding and stated: "that the financial responsibility for physical education and/or athletic and recreational programs be assumed by the institution".

The administrative directions taken by athletic programs at all Canadian universities were influenced by the "Matthews Report". The University of Alberta, as one example, has inculcated into its Department of Athletic Services the majority of the report's recommendations. Some other institutions have continued or adopted similar programs to Alberta. Others have made major or minor adjustments to their programs based on the report. Examples of present modeling would be as follows:

1. R. Tait McKenzie model. Function of physical education (or other name) with director (coordinator) of athletics responsible to dean (director) of physical education.

   University of Alberta
   University of Calgary
   University of Lethbridge

University of Saskatchewan
University of Regina
University of Manitoba
Laurentian University
McMaster University
University of Western Ontario
University of Windsor
Brock University
Queen's University
Concordia University
University of New Brunswick
University of New Brunswick, St. John
Universite de Moncton
Memorial University
University of British Columbia   )
York University   ) high similarity
Acadia University   )

2. Joint title with athletic prominence with some physical education or recreation emphasis:

Brandon University
University of Winnipeg
Carleton University
Sir Wilfrid Laurier
Mount Allison University
Mount Saint Vincent
University of Prince Edward Island
Saint Thomas   )
Ryerson   ) modifications of 2
Trent   )

3. Autonomous athletic department without or minimum coordinated relationship with physical education:

University of Victoria
Lakehead University
University of Toronto
University of Guelph
University of Waterloo
McGill University
Bishop's University
St. Francis Xavier University
St. Mary's University
Dalhousie University

4.   Quebec model, greater community role:

     Universite de Montreal
     Universite du Quebec, Trois Rivieres
     Universite de Sherbrooke
     Universite du Quebec, Chicoutimi
     Universite du Quebec, Rimouski
     Laval University

5.   Military Model:

     College Militaire Royale, Saint-Jean
     Royal Military College, Kingston

     The above lists are not intended to be exhaustive or definitive, but are only broad groupings of administrative variations used in facilitating university athletics.

     Three differing models from that of Alberta will be used as examples. Laval as the emerging community model; University of Toronto as an autonomous athletic department with additional administrative roles; and the various reporting structures should be noted in the UBC model which is yet another paradigm. Given that communication is a master process those, different models, work as well as the communication networks of the department and their respective universities permit. The model structure, in and of itself, is not paramount, communication and the relationship of the university to role of athletics is key to a positive and educationally sound program.

Issues

     There have been many issues that have arisen during the past twelve years related to the aforementioned models. These issues can cause much administrative pain at many levels within the university structure. Six of these will be examined briefly as an introduction to improved operation.

1.   Bifurcation of reporting; or too many vice-presidents in the soup. Reporting through one vice-president would do much to simplify reporting and budgeting in this many facetted program, i.e., Alberta.

2.   Movement of programming towards community; or how much is too much? This function has exploded during the past decade and many administrations have encouraged it for good and sometimes not so good reasons, i.e., Laval has been a leader in the sound planning of such programs. Where do they fit in your university structure?

3. Management of facilities; or who has the key? The combination of a
    positive appreciation and thorough knowledge of the various pro-
    grams combined with management skills is essential in these often
    most used of university facilities.

4. The internal stress to modify models in relationship to the per-
    ceived mandate of the university; or you're not part of the core.
    The entrenchment process that began for many universities at the
    time of the Matthews report has made it most difficult to initiate
    any hard money changes in the broad area of athletics and recre-
    ation.

5. The role of alumnae, and other non-university representatives on advisory
    committees related to athletics. Directly or indirectly the general
    direction of advisory representation has been to move more to policy
    involvement or to not be interested.

6. Who the Hell is the CIAU anyway?" This quote taken from a . . . of
    Canadian university _____ is not atypical of the frustrations
    that have occurred in recent years on Canadian campuses with
    respect to athletic lines of communication. The answer to the
    question is that CIAU is all of us.

There are concerns among Canadian university boards of governors,
administration, faculty and students with certain situations in Canadian
interuniversity athletics. Too often a joint meeting such as this has
been little more than a social gathering where underlying problems have
not surfaced. Twelve years have gone by since the Matthews Report was
published; times have changed, concerns must be heard, and solutions
planned.

Communication Futures

The nature and place of athletic programs on the campuses of
universities across this nation will doubtless undergo a degree of
metaphorosis over the coming decades. The form that this change assumes
will be determined by a fairly wide range of decision-makers but central
among them will be the presidents, deans and directors of athletic
programs. It seems to us that soundly developed and maintained lines of
communication will be of paramount importance if these changes are to be
managed within a broadly acceptable frame of reference. A communication
process is vital to gain this end. The following potential devices
might be considered as mechanisms to achieve open communication
channels.

Joint Committee. The creation of a six person committee comprised of two
members from each of the president's association, the CIAU and the CCUPEA
could serve as a useful filter to allow important messages to move among the
three groups. Such a group need meet only once or twice per year (or could be

called to deal with vital issues which might emerge from time to time). The committee could also serve as an important buffer among the groups should conflict arise insomuch as a bond of trust and understanding frequently builds within a group which meets on a regular basis.

Quarterly Comminique. In view of the number of special events, actions and even policy developments which occur within the CIAU each year it might be beneficial to the Presidents and to the CCUPEA if a one page quarterly comminique (issue driven) was produced by the CIAU.

Presidential Observes to the CIAU. While we realize the tremendous time limitation of each president we believe that an invitation should be extended to two university presidents to attend the annual CIAU meetings as observers. These invitees would be from campuses in close proximity to the CIAU annual meeting venue which would allow for a "drop-in" situation at low travel cost. All appropriate documentation from the CIAU meeting would be prepared for the observers prior to the meeting dates to allow for its perusal and an opportunity for the observe to be selective in their attendance.

Presidential Selection of CIAU Representatives. Each year, the presidents receive documentation from the CIAU office pertinent to the annual CIAU meeting and including a request to name the university's voting representative to the meetings themselves. Most presidents use this opportunity to discuss agenda items with their appointees and to review their university's stance on vital issues. We would encourage a wide-spread use of this strategy in that it provides for another important personal linkage between the chief executive officers of the universities and their CIAU representatives as well as a means of heightening awareness of the important place that the CIAU annual meeting has in the overall operation of the university.

Summary

The delivery systems of athletic programs within and among the universities of the vastness of Canada have a long and proud history. They have been shaped to fit the geo-political nature of a given region, the history of a university, the cultural ethos of a province but only to a limited degree the motive forces of significant outside agencies (e.g., the alumni, government agencies). The CIAU is an important element in the infrastructure of the AUCC and this is a fact that must, from time to time, be recalled. The member units of the CIAU have a wealth of diversity but that diversity is mainly subjugated to the overarching need to provide the highest possible quality of athletic opportunity to the student athletes through interuniversity competition. To ensure that their competitions are built on a strong philosophical basis requires the operation of a well-honed communication system.

References

Huzinga, Johan. (1950 translation of 1938 original). Homo Ludens, A Study of the Play - Element in Culture. Boston: The Beacon Press.

Macintosh, D.D. (1986) Issues in Canadian Sport (Chapter 10 of text to be published by University Press).

Matthews, A.W. (1974) Athletics in Canadian Universities. Ottawa: The Association of Universities and Colleges in Canada.

Nisetich, Frank J. (1980) Pindar's Victory Songs. Baltimore: The John Hopkins University Press.

Sandys, Sir John. (1915) The Odes of Pindar. Cambridge: Harvard University Press.

SECTION 2. THE ROLE OF INTERUNIVERSITY ATHLETICS: A
PRESIDENT'S APPROACH

- THE ROLE AND PLACE OF UNIVERSITY ATHLETICS IN A LARGE
  CANADIAN UNIVERSITY -- G.E. CONNELL

- THE ROLE OF ATHLETICS IN A MARITIME UNIVERSITY -- G.A. MCKINNON

- THE ROLE OF ATHLETICS IN A QUEBEC UNIVERSITY -- J-G. OUELLET

- DISCUSSION -- L. MALONEY

THE ROLE AND PLACE OF UNIVERSITY ATHLETICS
IN A LARGE CANADIAN UNIVERSITY

GEORGE E. CONNELL

At the University of Toronto, intercollegiate sport is part of a comprehensive, broadbased athletic program. This program is the largest extracurricular activity on campus, and is viewed by the University as an important aspect of the educational experience it offers its students. While much of the program is essentially recreational, the intercollegiate program is designed for students with a serious interest in sport excellence.

For your information, attached to this paper as Appendix A are (1) the University's Athletics Policy Objectives, which have been approved by the Governing Council, (2) some basic data regarding the intercollegiate program and, (3) the criteria used to decide levels of support for various intercollegiate sports.

Intercollegiate athletes are encouraged to make a commitment to both academic and athletic excellence. However, our firm view is that students are, first and foremost, students and their academic commitments must take priority. This principle underlies the whole of the University's educational program, including athletics. It is reflected in the reporting structure for athletics, which is through the University's academic vice-president. So as to ensure that there are no institutional inducements to place sport commitments before athletic ones, participation is completely voluntary. No scholarships or financial incentives are offered. No concessions in terms of admission, academic or degree requirements are made. Recruiting practices by athletic staff are carefully monitored. While the University is proud of its excellent athletic program and wants prospective students to be aware of its quality when the consider attending the University of Toronto, the emphasis in recruiting is on the provision of information. Coaches are firmly discouraged from trying to persuade prospective students to attend the University for mainly athletic reasons.

The University recognizes that student athletes may need assistance in maintaining both their academic and athletic commitments, and that the University has a responsibility in this area. An orientation program is mounted for intercollegiate athletes, along with special study skills programs offered by the staff of the University's Counselling and Learning Skills Service and the University Library. A senior member of the Department is responsible for counselling intercollegiate athletes regarding their academic progress. This is monitored through direct access to the University's academic records system. The need for special test and examination arrangements is recognized, but these are carefully controlled. Only the coordinator of intercollegiate athletics is authorized to make such arrangements with academic departments. Individual coaches may not do so. And, finally, the University's coaching staff are selected on the basis of their commitment to the University's philosophy regarding the place of athletics in the student experience at the University of Toronto, as well as their ability to develop the athletic skills of student athletes. It is expected that in all their interactions with students, they will reflect the educational emphasis of the University's athletic program.

Inter-university athletics involves a relationship with other universities for athletic competition purposes, and we believe that the nature of these relationships is an important factor in the quality of our athletic program and its fulfillment of its educational purposes. In the University's view, the most appropriate competitive relationships are with other institutions that share our academic and athletic philosophy, and are committed to athletic programs of comparable breadth and quality. We see no educational value in having our student athletes beat, or be beaten by, competitors whose skill level is radically different from theirs because of differential academic standards or athletic program quality. In fact, such competitive discrepancies may be an inducement to compromise the principles to which we are committed. Competitive alignments are also important because of their impact on schedules, which should be compatible with student athletes' academic priorities.

For some time, the University of Toronto has questioned whether its competitive relationships within the two Ontario university athletic leagues are appropriate. In spite of the establishment of a commission to oversee inter-university athletics in Ontario, this concern remains. It applies as well to national competition, in which we wish to be involved provided that there is a consensus among participating institutions regarding the role of university sport and the principles that should govern it.

In the past, inter-collegiate sport was a major force at the University of Toronto in terms of campus spirit and alumni loyalty. This is less true today, and to some extent this is regrettable. While we are endeavouring to revive interest in intercollegiate sport on campus because of its capacity to support a sense of community, this will not be done at the expense of intercollegiate athletes. Similarly, revenue generation is not a major issue in our intercollegiate program. Current gate receipts cover only a fraction of the cost of the intercollegiate program itself. We would welcome additional revenue, but are not prepared to compromise our view that the major beneficiaries of the intercollegiate program should be the student athletes themselves. Corporate support is another area with which we are prepared to become involved up to a point, but not if it becomes exploitive of our program or the interests of our student athletes.

Aside from the question of competitive alignments and scheduling which I have already mentioned, as an institution we are confronting a number of other issues involving our intercollegiate athletic program. Scarcity of financial and facility resources are forcing hard program choices upon us. Within the total athletic program, broad based high participation programs are being weighed against those in which few students take part. Given the relatively small number of student athletes involved in the intercollegiate program, this debate is an important one for intercollegiate sport. Within the intercollegiate program itself, we are struggling with the question of maintaining program breadth, that is, number of sports, as opposed to concentrating on program quality. Our present thinking is to emphasize the latter. There is also the matter of support for newer sports, in which interest is developing, as opposed to the more traditional ones.

The issue of support for women's programs is receiving careful attention. The University is committed to equality of opportunity in sports for members of both sexes, although there are some problems regarding application of this principle that remain to be resolved. The management structure of our department is fully integrated and, in fact, the coordinator of intercollegiate athletics is female. While many aspects of the total athletic program are co-educational, including intramural competition, so far co-ed competition at the inter-university level has not been endorsed, and was specifically rejected recently by our intercollegiate athletes themselves.

The role of high performance sport is another area of concern. The benefits to student athletes who are interested in international competition as well as the spill-over benefits to our athletic program generally that can occur as a result of collaboration with Sport Canada and the sport governing bodies are apparent. At the same time, just as with our intercollegiate competitive relationships, we are concerned that our involvement with high performance sport not distort the priorities of our athletic program or our student athletes. Therefore we are monitoring our involvement in this area with great care.

In closing I would like to compliment the Canadian Council of the University of Physical Education Administrators for taking the initiative to organize this conference. Inter-university athletics is a significant force in Canadian universities and the educational experience of our students. The educational philosophy which underlies our programs, their overall direction and their management deserve more careful attention than they often receive. I very much hope that as a result of today's discussions each of us will return to our institutions with a renewed commitment to ensuring that our athletics programs continue to operate in a manner which serves the best interests of our student athletes.

APPENDIX A

LEVELS OF SUPPORT FOR INTERCOLLEGIATE SPORTS

University of Toronto

Level I

- coach with a full-time appointment
- first priority for facility use within intercollegiate allocation for regular daily practice
- full practice and game gear other than footwear (except hockey)
- first priority for exhibition competition funds
- regular meals, transportation and lodging arrangements

Level II

- part-time coach with honorarium
- access to facilities for regular practice (3-4 per week)
- game uniforms
- second priority for exhibition competition funds within 250 mile radius
- regular meals, transportation and lodging arrangements

Level III

- part-time coach with nominal honorarium
- access to facilities for regular practice (3-4 per week) prior to championships
- game uniforms
- limited priority for exhibition competition funds
- regular meals, transportation and lodging arrangements

CRITERIA FOR DECIDING LEVEL OF SUPPORT FOR INDIVIDUAL SPORTS
(currently under review)

1. Participation

   A measure of the participation and interest in the sport on campus at various levels. Large numbers of students trying out for teams is a further indication of interest.

2. Appropriateness

   Sports whose schedules and season coincide with the academic year allowing for time to train and compete.

3. Facilities

The availability of a good facility on campus makes a significant difference to the quality of a program.

4. Coaching

Coaching is a crucial factor and the presence of a highly-rated coach is fundamental to a quality program.

5. Tradition

Some sports have a long history of success at the University of Toronto and are considered important to alumni and community alike.

University of Toronto
Athletics Policy Objectives
(in order of priority)

1. (a) The discipline of physical education

    To facilitate scholarly research into physical education and
    for the teaching of professional physical educators and
    community sports leaders.

    (b) Athletic instruction, competition and recreation

    To provide avocational instruction, physical recreation, and
    intramural, intercollegiate and other athletic competition for
    members of the University community and to integrate such
    programmes for men and women as much as possible.

    (c) Physical fitness

    To contribute to the continuing physical well-being of members
    of the University community by providing programmes that
    stress the values and hazards of physical fitness and by
    providing physical fitness testing and the prescription of
    exercise.

2. (a) Excellence in athletic performance

    To provide opportunity for outstanding athletes to pursue
    world standards of performance and to provide for empirical
    research into the requirements of excellence in selected
    sports.

    (b) Service to the neighbouring community

    To supplement recreation opportunities for members of the
    adjacent community by providing appropriate programmes on a
    regular basis in cooperation with the City of Toronto Depart-
    ment of Parks and Recreation.

    (c) Service to the extramural athletics community

    To supplement, where possible, opportunities for the Toronto
    athletics community to use University facilities for training,
    competition and special demonstrations.

    (d) Provisions for spectators

    To provide for spectator opportunities in competitive sports.

THE ROLE OF ATHLETICS IN A MARITIME UNIVERSITY

G.A. McKINNON

A famous heavyweight boxer once boarded an aircraft and as he took his seat the stewardess reminded him to fasten his seat belt. "Superman don't need no seat belt," replied the boxer. "Superman don't need no airplane, either," retorted the stewardess. He fastened his seat belt. Often when athletes and athletics at universities are mentioned, this erroneous stereotype of the illiterate, aggressive, and arrogant athlete comes to mind. This, of course, is a distortion, and I wish to make it clear at the outset that that is not my view of our student athletes. Still, the myth survives that academic excellence and superior athletic performance are incompatible. Whatever happened to mens sana in corpore sano? Perhaps this type of snobbery can be traced back to a distinguished president at Harvard University who frequently expressed misgivings about sport. At one point he announced at the end of a successful baseball season that he was thinking of dropping the sport. Pressed for an explanation, he said, "Well, this year I'm told the team did well because the pitcher has a fine curve ball. I understand that a curve ball is thrown with a deliberate attempt to deceive. Surely that is not an ability we should want to foster at Harvard." I shall try not to throw any curve balls -- or use any other device to deceive.

I thank you for the invitation to take part in this Conference on Interuniversity Athletics. I was not aware until I read the program that no fewer than five national groups are intimately involved in some aspects of university athletics. The Canadian Council of University Physical Education Administrators are to be commended for bringing representatives of these groups together for the first time. Co-operation and co-ordination can only be helpful to all of them.

The topic assigned to me is "The role of athletics in a Maritime university," I speak only for myself and of my own university, St. Francis Xavier University. With fewer than three thousand students we are among the small universities in Canada -- but we have established a healthy athletics program. Our teams have taken part in national championship games in all the major sports and have won championship games in basketball and football. We do not, however, consider national championships or the preparation of teams for that level of competition a priority. We are entirely satisfied to be competitive within our region, with occasionally a team in the nationals. We make a very deliberate effort to pitch our athletics program at a level that recognizes the important advantages that can be gained without adversely affecting our academic program.

Let us look briefly at these advantages. In a setting such as ours, I can identify at least four groups that benefit from a properly regulated sports program: the university, the alumni, the local community, and of course the participating students.

A proper program of athletics in a small residential university contributes to morale, school spirit, provides a focus for joint activity; it deepens the student's ties with the school and engenders co-operative effort. It is not uncommon at Maritime universities to have several thousand spectators attend a basketball game, or a hockey game. Such events have a notable, almost tangible influence on morale and spirit that spill over into every aspect of student life.

Every successful university needs a dynamic, loyal alumni association to help it maintain its traditions, to assist in recruiting superior students and to represent the university in society. No single activity helps to enliven more alumni loyalty than a good sports program. An alumnus who is a surgeon with a busy practice described for me the torture he endures from his colleagues in the O.R. when our team has lost a game. His recompense comes when we win. So alumni relations is not a trivial matter, and athletics keep interest high.

At St. Francis Xavier University, we have a long tradition of involvement in the local community. Antigonish is a town of about 6000 and we are the largest employer in the area. We depend on the town, and the town depends on us. A delicate symbiotic relationship has evolved in which again sporting activities are important. The good burghers of Antigonish identify with us and our teams and have become strong supporters of all aspects of university life.

The student who participates in a well-run athletics program also derives many benefits. Quite apart from honing his or her skills as an athlete, there are the invaluable lessons of self-mastery, discipline, learning to deal with the heights of adulation, and the depths of rejection, the development of poise and self-confidence, and the achievement of goals. The successful interuniversity athlete must be involved in the pursuit of excellence, surely an important pursuit for every student.

But there are dangers and pitfalls that must be carefully avoided. The varsity athletes must not become an elite upon whom all resources are spent. There must be a balance between intramural physical recreation and athletics programs and the inter-university activity. They should be mutually supportive, not in competition.

The varsity athlete must be a student first. No exception to the school's admission standards should be tolerated, and no lowering of academic standards can be countenanced for continuing students who play on varsity teams. When athletes are permitted to carry less than a full academic load in any year, that student is being used or abused by the university. We require all student athletes to carry five full courses in each academic year.

I believe we are <u>atypical</u> in this requirement. If this regulation was enforced universally in Canada, many abuses would be eliminated.

I need not say that special financial deals for athletes are also an abuse. Bursary support must be administered by the Awards Office and should be as open as all other awards.

In order to avoid these and other problems, the presidents of all Atlantic universities involved in inter-university athletics have reconstituted the AUAA (Atlantic Universities Athletic Association) and now form the Board of Directors of that organization. This will permit the senior university administrators to set policy for the inter-university athletics competition. It would, in my view, be helpful if the CIAU were brought more closely under the supervision of the presidents. Standing somewhat removed from the arena, presidents should be better able than athletic directors to assure that the academic and the athletic are properly balanced. As an example, I am sure that most university presidents feel that this year's national championships are being held much too late in the year, too close to final examinations. Perhaps the Atlantic experience may in the years ahead be applied on the national scene.

In conclusion, may I summarize my position by citing four basic positions for inter-university athletics competition:

1. Athletics programs should be regarded as integral parts of the total educational program, and they should be conducted in a manner which will ensure that they are worthy of such consideration.

2. Inter-university athletics programs should supplement rather than compete with intramural athletics programs.

3. Inter-university athletics should be subject to the same administrative control as the total education program.

4. Inter-university athletics programs should be conducted in such a way that the physical and academic welfare of the participants be protected and fostered.

THE ROLE OF ATHLETICS IN A QUEBEC UNIVERSITY

J-G. OUELLET

One of the persistent problems, that has plagued institutions of higher education in Canada throughout the years, has been defining the role that athletics should assume on the campuses of this Country. To comprehend the dilemma of many institutions, it is imperative that one understands the evolutionary development of athletics in Canada and, more particularly, in Quebec.

Interuniversity athletics originated and flourished as a student-initiated, non-educational, extra-curricular activity. It was only institutional concern about the direction of such programs that led to the creation of athletic associations or councils with institutional, student and, often, alumni representation.

In 1923, the Committee of Athletics of Canadian Universities recognized the need to specify the purpose and role of athletics in higher education institutions in Canada.

This committee proposed that interuniversity athletics programs had no place in higher education unless they were designed for student participation and educational outcomes rather than spectator entertainment, institutional prestige, and gate receipts. Thus, the educational potential and preferred role of such programs was formally stated.

However, in 1966 many different philosophies and methods were being utilized to organize, govern, finance, and staff athletic programs throughout Canada. This led the standing Committee for Physical Education and Athletics of the Association of Universities and Colleges of Canada to reaffirm the belief that athletic activity of students was a part of the total education experience of an institution of higher learning and to recommend a basic philosophical position (integrated physical education and athletic program) and operating principles to institutions.

In 1974, the Matthews Report, entitled "Athletics in Canadian Universities," was to re-evaluate the validity of the basic philosophical position and the pragmatic methodologies suggested in 1966 in comparison to the educational climate of 1974.

If we briefly analyze the evolution of athletics in Quebec, we can notice that most Quebec institutions have not adopted this philosophical position and have developed their inter and intra university sports and physical activity programs around a different organizational model. In fact, interuniversity sports in most Quebec institutions are under the responsibility of an administrative unit that has no structural or organic links with an academic unit. It is usually closely associated with, or directly part of, student services. This structure, which relies partly on student subsidization, acknowledges partial control of students in the governance of athletic programs which often produces, not only a lack of consistency in the administrative process, but also in the orientation of the programs. This may explain in part the different trends that Quebec universities have followed over the past 25 years.

In the 60's, most institutions, and particularly the francophone ones, had limited athletic facilities, and the sports administrators chose to privilege a restricted number of interuniversity sports and gave less attention to intramural sports.

The 70's were marked by the construction of sports facilities (Montreal - Laval - Sherbrooke), the establishment of the different campuses of the Universite du Quebec, and the era of "sport pour tous". Broader programs of individual activities and intramural sports were provided to enable as many students as possible to take part. Students demanded programs that were more compatible with the objectives that they were pursuing. These objectives can be summarized into four categories: initiation, competition, recreation, excellence (high level competition).

The consequences of this shift to mass participation resulted in reduced interuniversity competition (e.g., Montreal withdrew completely from interuniversity competition; Laval and Bishops dropped their interuniversity hockey program).

In the 80's, we witness a renewed interest in high level competition in many francophone institutions. There are definite signs that the development of excellence in sport seems to be regaining acceptance amongst students and university administrators. On the other hand, the increased level of performance in Quebec and in Canada has lead francophone institutions to specialize in certain sports in order to be competitive with their anglophone counterparts. As a result, only one francophone institution offers an interuniversity program in men's basketball (UQTR) and only one in women's basketball (LAVAL).

Growing budgetary restrictions have forced university administrators to revise their priorities and to determine the objectives and the scope of the sports and physical activity programs that would be offered by their institution. The need to provide for the complete education of both mind and body of all students in an academic institution also creates problems in light of the limited facilities often available to fulfill the needs of recreation and intramural activities and the increasing use of the university facilities by community groups and members.

These factors have influenced each institution differently. The model of anglophone institutions is based on older traditions and is centered around interuniversity programs in football, basketball and, to a lesser degree, ice hockey.

The evolution of the general model of sports organization in Quebec took place almost at the same time as the organization of interuniversity sport in Quebec. Consequently, the sport traditions in francophone institutions are less deeply rooted and reflect different realities.

It has become a complex operation when it becomes time to organize interuniversity competition between institutions who pursue different objectives in a particular sport or are involved in different sports. This problem is particularly acute when we deal with the important debate of the role that the university plays in high level competition or in the development of excellence in sport. The Quebec institutions that have chosen to develop excellence (that is to develop athletes who aspire to compete on our national team) have realized that they must work in partnership with sport governing bodies and other organizations (provincial and national) in order to play a contributing role.

Organization of interuniversity sports for that category of participants may have to be looked at in a different perspective and serious consideration will have to be given to opportunities for competition "outside their athletic associations".

To succeed in the pursuit of athletic excellence, participating institutions must provide full time coaching and conditions which will allow student athletes not only to further develop their talents but also to succeed academically.

Although we have seen considerable improvement in the above areas in the last decade, some important issues have yet to be resolved in relation to interuniversity competition. These include:

1. Present eligibility restrictions for interuniversity competition.
   - full load
   - number of years
   - part-time students

2. Competition with non-university organizations.

3. In team sports, participation of "non eligible" athletes in "open" competition.

4. Increasing pressure for self financing interuniversity programs.

5. Accommodation of community members facilities needs.

6. Limited number of institutions in a conference pursuing the same goals in a particular sport.

7. Growing necessity to adapt to the influence of external factors such as regional and national training centres that affect the interuniversity sports infrastructure.

The choices that each institution has decided to make as to the type of program it supports in interuniversity competition has created a complex sports chess-board. It is my belief that efforts with the "milieu" will now have to become more concerted and better coordinated if we want to provide students with athletic experiences which challenge their abilities while maximizing educational benefits.

This is our challenge for the 90's.

DISCUSSION ON "THE ROLE OF UNIVERSITY ATHLETICS:
A PRESIDENT'S PERSPECTIVE"

L. MALONEY, MODERATOR

Dr. Robert Morford: I have a question for Dr. Connell. During the course of your talk you made reference to the Division One style of athletics in the NCAA. I think you referred to these as being exploited rather than abetted. I wonder if you would elaborate on what the assumptions are which underlie the use of these terms.

Dr. George Connell: I am indebted to Earle Zeigler for my insight into some of the practices and problems with the NCAA. He has written extensively on the topic. I think most of the abuses of which I am aware were in football and basketball. In these sports, there is a prominence of athletes whose goals are clearly to qualify for the NFL or the NBA and I think the record there is pretty calamitous. That is, the number of students who enter university with scholarships and are heading in that direction is considerable. The number of those who actually succeed in acquiring a degree or even the rudiments of a satisfactory education is deplorably low. The particularly scandalous affair that I referred to has been fairly well documented and it seems to me that there is hardly an issue of the chronicles of higher education these days that doesn't cite a disaster in one school or another. One that I followed with some interest was the case at Tulane University. That is just a single incident and I am sure the members of the audience can cite many others. I think it would be a mistake to incriminate all the U.S. colleges. I think there are some outstanding programs and some fine universities which succeed in competing at a high level. I can cite Harvard and Stanford as two, perhaps the University of Michigan as a third. I meet quite frequently with the presidents of those universities and I am impressed by how much of their time and energy that the problem absorbs. I think this is a fairly recent development and as you may know there is now a committee of the Presidents which has assumed some responsibility in the NCAA. But, the problems seem to be chronic, something very difficult to come to grips with and solve. I think we are all aware of the kinds of issues that Craig McKinnon cited and the importance, for example, of athletic programs for alumni; that is a very strong binding force. Perhaps even more prominent is the television sports linkage that Don MacIntosh cited. This has become such an important source of revenue for some institutions that gaining exposure on the national networks and gaining the revenue that comes from it becomes one of the prime motives of the intercollegiate athletics program.

Dr. Murray Smith: I would like to address a question to the panel but I think Dr. McKinnon referred to this particular point. At the University of Alberta, we have a number of students who, for a variety of quite legitimate reasons extend the four year program over five or even six years. I wonder if, (I wouldn't certainly advocate this as a matter of course,) intercollegiate athletes shouldn't be encouraged to do this or be allowed to do it. Can you conceive of it being legitimate for certain athletes, who have a very strong desire to get a high quality education and also to perform to very high standards, the highest possible standards in athletics, that this extended time for a degree might be a legitimate consideration?

Dr. Greg McKinnon: I think the important principle is that special rules should not be made for athletes. There may be good reasons to dispense a given student from area overload. I can see that, but that kind of thing should not be exclusive to the athletic program or to the athlete. I think if athletics are to have credibility, we have to deal with all of our students as student first. Then, if there is some reason to make an exception, that kind of exception should be available to everyone, not just athletes.

Ms. Abby Hoffman: I promised myself I wasn't going to speak but I am. I am going to direct my question to Don McIntosh and perhaps also to President Connell. I feel that the role of a university is to promote excellence in academics. Do you not also see the role of a university to provide -- to provide, and that is the key word -- a program for the elite athlete who also wants to combine athletics with elitism in a university setting?

Dr. Greg MacKinnon: I don't think that I am the appropriate one to respond because I have absolutely no ambition to have that kind of a centre of excellence at my university. Perhaps it would be more appropriate for another panel member to comment.

Dr. Jean-Guy Ouellet: We will have to determine what elitism is in sport. At the Universite de Sherbrooke we have a certain number of athletes who are not in CIAU programs but are at the elite level. One, for example, -- I am talking about speed skating -- one of our top skaters in Canada is on a special program trying to combine academic work and also excel in sports. The academic load is distributed over three semesters as opposed to two semesters. This student is not capable of following the normal load, due to sport commitments on a semester basis but is capable of following the normal load on a yearly basis. We try to encourage this type of program, but it should not be done on a full scale or a team basis.

Dr. George Connell: I think universities can and should accommodate individuals who have the potential to be outstanding international athletes, but I really have grave doubts about those individuals planning their prime athletic training and competitive experience within the normal university competitive environment. If athletes are prepared to commit the time and energy that is necessary to compete at the international level, my guess would be that in most cases they are not going to be able to satisfy academic requirements and be full time students at the same time. And I think if the university program is shaped exclusively to accommodate those kinds of individuals, we would end up doing a great disservice to other students and to the normal priorities of the university's academic and athletic programs.

Dr. Larry Maloney: Let me again say thank you to the three Presidents. When the CCUPEA began discussion about the possibility of this kind of conference, we felt it was absolutely necessary to have the perspective from the university Presidents. We want to say thank you very much for taking the time out of your very busy schedules to prepare the thought provoking comments you have given us today.

SECTION 3.   EXTERNAL FACTORS AFFECTING INTERUNIVERSITY ATHLETICS

- THE EFFECT OF INTERNATIONAL SPORT ON CANADIAN INTERUNIVERSITY
  ATHLETICS -- R. JACKSON

- THE EFFECT OF EXTERNAL FACTORS ON ATHLETICS FROM AN ACADEMIC
  PERSPECTIVE -- M. KEYES

- DISCUSSION -- S. ROBBINS

THE EFFECT OF INTERNATIONAL SPORT ON
CANADIAN INTERUNIVERSITY ATHLETICS

R. JACKSON

In a word, international sport in the last few years has had an extraordinary influence on Canadian interuniversity athletics.

With the dramatic evolution of the federal government's support of national-level sport through the 1970's and into the 1980's, (a pattern followed by a few provincial governments), there has been a large infusion of new funding for national and international sport. In the early 70's, the federal contribution rose slowly between $5 - $10 million dollars. Currently, the federal government spends 4-5 times this amount each year, sponsoring national team programs. Much of this funding directly or indirectly affects Canadian university sport.

How has Canada's international sport programme influenced intercollegiate sport? First, university administrators, coaches, athletes, and other officials have gained first-class experiences as a result of their involvement with expanded national and international programs.

Second, competition opportunities outside of the intercollegiate program for university athletes and coaches have broadly expanded, and include, in a regular four year cycle, the World Student Games, the Pan American Games, the Olympic Summer and Winter Games, the Commonwealth Games, and many international tours.

Third, there has been an evolution in philosophy amongst sport administrators at universities -- one that has also evolved for Canadian teams. Striving for excellence appears to be an acceptable goal now for intercollegiate sport.

Fourth, coaching is considerably improved at the Universities, partly because there are more opportunities for university coaches to be involved with national and international projects, and partly because there is more funding from the federal and provincial governments to provide salaries to support full-time coaches.

Fifth, university athletes are stronger and more experienced than they have been in the past, particularly in the developing sports such as swimming, volleyball, gymnastics, and the like. These athletes have more opportunity for provincial and national level experiences, including provincial championships and games, and The Canada Games. The athletes receive more financial support than before, because of the national carded athlete program.

Sixth, the sport scientists and sport medical personnel at universities are more active and experienced and in greater numbers, partly because of the strong development of their own professional organizations, and partly because of the greater opportunities provided for international experience.

Seventh, the stimulation of the Coaching Association of Canada in developing educational programs for coaches, and encouraging a respectable coaching profession in Canada, have led to better training and an improved professional status for full-time coaches.

Eighth, many universities have benefited from the provision of world-class facilities, as a result of major games, or federal and provincial government contributions to upgrade facilities to world-class standards. These facilities have often resulted from commitments by government to improve opportunities for Canada's national athletes.

It is not surprising that universities have benefited from the extra-ordinary development of Canada's national sport system -- a system in it's undeveloped stage in the 1960's that saw Canadian teams regularly finishing 25th - 30th at Olympic Games. The current system has improved so dramatically, that Canada finished 4th out of 143 nations at the Los Angeles Olympic Games, with 44 medals, 10 of them Gold.

However, the title of this talk could as easily be "The Effect of Canadian Interuniversity Athletics on International Sport" because Canadian universities have contributed enormously to this achievement.

Indeed, in the last 25 years, universities have been regular and important contributors to the development of Canada's international athletes for reasons that are readily understandable:

1. Universities have had the finest high performance sport facilities in their communities.

2. In the 1960's and into the 1970's, universities provided almost the only opportunity for coaches to be hired on a part-time or full-time basis, and these coaches tended to be the best in the community.

3. Universities had sports administrative and technical expertise which was often lacking in volunteer organizations.

4. Universities have developed the best sport teams in a province, in sports such as hockey, basketball, volleyball, wrestling, rowing, and so on.

5. Many faculty members have had the opportunity to provide service to assist amateur sport.

What are the advantages to the university for having an involvement with international sport programs?

1. Universities, who try to acquire full-time coaching for their intercollegiate programs and teaching for their undergraduate programs, often find a partial salary arrangement with an outside sport organization the only answer to having full-time expertise.

2. There are research and athlete testing opportunities for sport science laboratories.

3. The quality of the intercollegiate sports program is often improved by having a nationally experienced coach develop the university's athletes.

4. Many national teams rent university facilities and purchase a variety of university services.

5. The affiliation of world-class coaches and athletes with a Faculty of Physical Education and its students should be of real benefit to those studying the training of athletes.

6. Undergraduate and graduate programs in physical education that emphasize a coaching science component, benefit from affiliation with international caliber coaches and athletes.

However, there are reasons that have discouraged universities from developing a relationship with national and international level sport.

1. Often, there are not adequate training facilities that can be made available to outside groups.

2. The time requirements for training international athletes are so extensive, that there is conflict for use of facilities between intercollegiate sport, academic programs, recreational programs and these athletes.

3. There is a cost to the university for supporting these national team programs, in indirect terms (light, heat, etc.) and in direct terms.

4. Many universities will not have the interest in spending considerable time to work out relationships with national sport agencies. They are interested in developing their academic and sport programs in other directions.

THE EFFECT OF EXTERNAL FACTORS ON ATHLETICS
FROM AN ACADEMIC PERSPECTIVE

MARY E. KEYES

In this presentation, the effect of some external factors will be discussed as they impact on athletics from an academic perspective; for example, the effect of high performance sport centres promoted by Sport Canada, community demands, sponsorship, television contracts, and legislation. By no means should this list be thought to be exhaustive, rather it represents those external factors which have occupied the attention of the Canadian Intercollegiate Athletic Union (CIAU) in their Annual General Meetings and which have prompted recommendations resulting in new policies and procedures within this organization. Unfortunately, the academic ramifications of the proposed regulation changes have not always been considered.

High Performance Sport Centres

Let's begin by discussing two or three potential problems which could develop when an external factor such as a high performance sport centre sponsored by Sport Canada is established on campus. One issue which needs to be addressed by both the athlete and the university is whether it is possible for an individual to excel in university academics and simultaneously participate internationally in a sport; ultimately both parties must address what compromise is to be made in order to attempt each. Each one of us is able to give excellent examples of individual international athletes who have gained a university education while at the same time representing their country in the sports arena - Abby Hoffman and Roger Jackson are two prime examples. These individuals competed at the highest level of competition in their sport and, at the same time pursued and received well respected university degrees.

However, today it is difficult for most individuals to be both a full-time student and an elite athlete; for many, these goals are not compatible. It was for this reason, that the CIAU passed a new eligibility regulation which required a student to be enrolled in a minimum of 9 units rather than 18 units per year for competition in interuniversity sport. This new regulation recognizes that it is difficult, if not impossible, for elite athletes to maintain a full academic load, to train, and to compete at the international level. The passage of this regulation, however, signaled a shift in emphasis in both the interuniversity athletic programme and the academic conditions required of all athletes. I do not quarrel with elite athletes spreading their academic programme over several years in order to participate at an elite level in sport but I do become concerned if this becomes the practice of all athletes.

This leads into an examination of the university requirements for establishing a high performance sport centre. Quoting from the "High Performance Sport Centre Criteria" (1983).

"Athletes must have access to as complete a spectrum of educational opportunities as possible . . . The educational institutions must offer flexible programming in terms of variety and availability of courses as well as flexibility of timing" (p.5).

It must be understood and appreciated by both the athlete and the sports governing body when establishing a high performance sport centre on a campus that "flexibility" within the academic programme does not mean two standards of education -- one for the elite athlete and a different one for the regular undergraduate student. Flexibility means that a student athlete may not take a full load each term, it may mean that examinations are rescheduled to accommodate the athlete's travel and competition conflicts, it may mean that timetables are modified to accommodate the training schedules of athletes, or it may mean that instead of completing a degree in four years it is completed in five or six years. Flexibility does not mean that the athlete does not meet the same academic standards as any other student in individual courses or in a programme of study. It does not mean that entrance or graduation standards are adjusted for athletes in a manner which is different from procedures used for other students. Flexibility is needed to be sure but compromising academic standards should not be condoned by any of us. We have vivid examples south of our border of the problems extant in high education when only lip service has been paid to academic standards for athletes. The maintenance of academic rigor is the responsibility of the faculty in each institution. High performance sport centres will not challenge academic credibility unless we permit them to do so. We need not compromise these standards even for elite athletes in our high performance sports centres as we attempt to provide the necessary flexibility for them as they combine their sport and academic pursuits.

High performance sports centres add much to our campus. The role model provided by elite athletes pursuing a degree sets a standard of achievement which is consistent with the quest for excellence in all our university endeavours. The opportunity for our sport science faculty to pursue research in areas of their own interest using high calibre athletes as subjects is beneficial. The opportunity to share coaching expertise is also a university benefit. I support high performance sport centres at our universities if the conditions of their establishment are clearly delineated and well understood by all involved.

Our institutions are under attack. At the same time that government financial support to our universities is diminishing, societal expectations of universities is increasing. These pressures are also being applied in athletics. Communities, sports governing bodies, governments and athletes expect more and better services provided by the physical education and athletic departments. Our researchers are expected to be available to provide fitness appraisal and training services, our gymnasia, swimming pools and weight rooms are expected to be available free of charge around the clock for high school and community athletes' use. Our sports medicine personnel and facilities are seen as a community resource. Our coaches and teaching faculty are expected to be available on request to speak at professional development days and athletic banquets and to play leadership roles in many minor sport groups or government committees. To be sure these are community service responsibilities we acknowledge and accept readily but for a cost. The cost, if we accept too many requests, is that we spread ourselves too thinly and, therefore, are forced by the limitation of time to reduce our attention and energies toward achieving a level of excellence in our athletic pursuits. As a consequence, as coaches and teachers in sport, dance, and exercise, we are not at the cutting edge of new developments. One of the most difficult decisions to be undertaken in our university athletic departments among faculty is to establish priorities and to determine our responsibilities for service both internally and externally. Before we allow ourselves to be all things to all people, we must know what our athletic mission is, how we are to accomplish it, and how to protect ourselves as we work to meet our determined goals. "No" may become an important word in our vocabulary if we are to withstand some external pressures which are not seen to be our primary mission.

Financial Implications: Sponsorship and Contracts

The financial constraints pressuring our university administrators and faculty has meant that recent decisions have been taken regarding publicity and athletic sponsorship. Those decisions have had a profound effect on how we conduct athletics. As budgets have been reduced, the pressure to maintain programme has prompted everyone associated with athletics to become involved with fund raising. Our liaisons with breweries and tobacco companies, the easiest corporate sponsors to obtain, has challenged us to rationalize the conflicting messages we are portraying relating to lifestyle and sport versus the need to obtain scarce dollars. What is the academic and athletic costs of the benefits received from these sponsorship dollars?

Not only are corporate dollars a necessity in our athletic programmes of the 1980's but so too is the publicity received through television coverage. It has been suggested by some that our university's are being judge by their athletic programmes as portrayed on TSN. To be ranked nationally, to have key games televised, and to bring our university to the attention of the public has ramifications too complex to dwell upon in this presentation. But it must be acknowledged that although television exposure is a vehicle for showcasing our institutions (and naturally each of us wants to make the best presentation possible), our packaging and our potential for publicity is being given more important and serious consideration than is the effect of television coverage on our athletes' academic considerations. To perform well before the television cameras has added extra pressures for both our athletes and coaches. The concept "more is better" is being promoted -- more practice is needed, more exhibition games are necessary, more tournaments are required, more money is needed. However, more is not better when these additional sport demands impinge upon an athlete's ability to pursue an undergraduate programme. For example, to maximize television coverage and revenue, the CIAU National Championships in hockey are scheduled for the weekend of March 23rd. This schedule leaves less than a month for students to prepare for final examinations. Television coverage is not more important from my perspective than having a schedule during the year which accommodates the academic needs of our athletes.

I would challenge athletic administrators to re-read the minutes of your recent CIAU meetings and to do a content analysis of the time expended on discussions of high performance sport centres, sponsorship, and television contracts in comparison to considerations which have a direct bearing on the academic mission of athletes in institutions of higher learning. External pressures such as these have overshadowed our primary mission of providing good competition in an educational environment which is different from both provincial and national sports governing bodies and professional sport competitions. It is essential that the university set its own policies and procedures which will protect its mission in athletics. Otherwise, the master of interuniversity athletics will be the owners of sponsorship dollars -- whether the private sector or government.

Women's Issues

In conclusion, I want to discuss one final example of an external factor which should be having an impact on our athletic programmes. That is the Constitution. The Women's Committee of the CIAU, in its recent study, has provided evidence that since 1978 there has been a decrease in opportunity of leadership for women as coaches and administrators, the competitive opportunities for our women athletes are less than for our male athletes, and I would suggest that if a study of per capita funding for our men's and women's programmes were undertaken the women would be seen to have less funding as well. This lack of equity in our athletic programmes must be corrected if we do not want an external factor such as a court challenge confronting us. In our academic environment, we attempt to protect the rights of all individuals; we should not be satisfied with less in our athletic programmes.

Concluding Remarks

Athletics is a dynamic phenomenon in our university and we need to continually reassess its role. External pressures are here to stay. Each institution will deal with them in its own way. I do not want to suggest that every university in Canada should accept the same mission statement, goals and objectives for athletics. What I am saying is that every university must be aware of what its goals and objectives are and pursue them vigorously. For some universities, the programme in athletics may be the entertainment model, for others, the participation model; for some, only a few elite sports will be supported, for others, a broadly based programme will be offered. Universities must establish their own programmes, and protect their own autonomy. Then, and only then, will they be able to deal logically and consistently with external pressures which will affect how their interuniversity programmes develop. Uniformity is not the answer, leagues among institutions with common philosophies will develop. Academic credibility is essential, for all however, if sport is to be maintained within our institutions of higher learning.

Reference

High Performance Sport Centres General Criteria. Ottawa: Government of Canada, 1983.

DISCUSSION ON "EXTERNAL FACTORS AFFECTING
INTERUNIVERSITY ATHLETICS"

S. ROBBINS, MODERATOR

Dr. Stu Robbins: This morning Abby Hoffman indicated to us the challenge involved with Sport Canada and High Performance Sports. Roger Jackson spoke about the benefits which may accrue from international sport participation and Mary Keyes alerted us to some of the dangers and pitfalls we can fall into as we move in some of these directions. Perhaps we could move immediately then into some questions and discussion which we might have for the panel and encourage some interaction among the participants.

Dr. Tom Meninger: I would like to address Miss Hoffman. If my notes are correct, at one point in your excellent talk this morning , you made a passing reference to universities thinking they are a domain unto themselves. The fact of the matter is universities think like that, rightly or wrongly in trying to sort out some high performance issues. At our university, this can be very very complex and raise all sorts of delicate issues. I wonder whether Sport Canada and equivalent organizations are sufficiently attentive in their dealings, in their negotiations with universities, of talking with the Presidents or the chief academic officers, in some cases maybe with academic Senates and so forth? I wonder whether there might be some room for improvement in that area of activity? Now I am taking some risk in asking this question because perhaps you do it already and I'm just completely ignorant about it.

Ms Abby Hoffman: That's a very good question. I think the response to it is that in a formal or ongoing sense, that kind of communication and dialogue does not tend to occur. Two reasons come to mind. One is there isn't often a venue or forum for that kind of discussion. Our main link with the university system on any sort of organizational scale is with the CIAU, I made the point this morning about the CIAU having a more limited mandate than what is required in terms of a party with whom we should have that discussion. We know in advance that there is tremendous variance from one university to the next in terms of the senior administration. In a number of cases, we have had very good projects brought forward to us with the full endorsement and support of the university President and key Vice-Presidents at that institution. And in those cases, there may be discussion with the senior management or perhaps there may not be any need for discussion. In other instances, without telling tales out of school here, the people with whom we deal in the university are pursuing something that is at cross purposes with the senior administration. Let's put it this way; they might be taking some

---

* Paper not submitted for publication

initiatives that are better left to the more junior ranks of the university hierarchy. And so we proceed with them to work through the details of the project, put it into place, and as long as the ripples aren't too extreme in the university, the project goes on.

Dr. Donald MacIntosh: Let me comment very briefly. That last thing you were talking about might be counterproductive to everyone's interest. Maybe, just maybe, and I recognize the validity of the university responsibility, but if Sport Canada, before it made a decision to go ahead, insisted on us having the President's signature on the dotted line, that might be helpful?

Ms. Abby Hoffman: I can't help but agree with that comment. I guess the only footnote I would add to that is perhaps for good reasons, perhaps not, University athletics often do not occupy enough of the time and energy of the Senate, President, Vice-presidents, and so on, I think it is perhaps fair to conclude that there isn't always a consistent line of thinking in any one institution. All the kinds of diversity of opinions expressed here today may be operating in any one given institution on any day. But, your point is well taken.

Dr. Ed Enos to Mary Keyes: You made reference to leadership roles increasing for women. Could you give me the reference for that?

Dr. Mary Keyes: It's a CIAU women's program study. There was a preliminary one and then there was one that was conducted for the period from 1978 to 1984.

Dr. Ed Enos: Do you know the percentages?

Dr. Mary Keyes: I would have to go to the study. They studied only leadership and participation. At my own institution, I did a per capita analysis of all our sports and we have got a problem.

Dr. Ed Enos: Can you give me McMaster's statistics then?

Dr. Mary Keyes: Well, in certain sports we have more money per capita going into women's sports, such as women's volleyball, but on a general basis, our men's sports receive significantly higher support on a per capita basis. Now you have got problems with football and hockey being included, but I think that that's an issue that we really have to look at. I think we should look at per diem costs being similar, equipment costs being similar, those types of things that we can really control. If we try to address those inequities, then we have come a long way in solving the problem.

Unidentified Speaker: Dr. Keyes made the point about the change from the traditional university in the context of sports. I think the changes in the traditions of the university as a whole are moving so quickly that in fact some of the comments you made find themselves redundant very quickly. I am referring particularly to the move toward part time study at the university level which is increasing. Very soon a very significant percentage of our instruction might be for part time individuals and the flexibility that is required to process those cases is such that some institutions, my own included, find that you can take one course a year for the rest of your life and get your degree. The result is that in fact, we are putting greater academic demands on our athletes than on any other group of students by requiring them to maintain a particular credit level whereas at the moment the concern might be that athletes might take less than the required loads than the average student. And that is the case at Simon Fraser University; that our requirements in terms of load are higher for athletes than any other type of student.

Dr. Mary Keyes: I agree. I think our part-time students are disadvantaged in that they can't participate in intercollegiate programs, but the concern that I have is that you could change the whole focus of intercollegiate athletics to a part-time endeavour. A student will make athletics a full-time endeavour and the academic requirement such a minimal part time endeavour that the whole quota of time spent in sports will change. And then the ordinary student won't want to participate in athletics because they won't want to be at the university for seven or eight years to get their degree.

Ms. Joyce Fromson: You talked about domain. The university is funded by a grant commission which is under the Minister of Education. The provincial sport governing body is funded by money under the provincial Minister of Sport. The national sport governing bodies are funded under the Federal Minister of Sport. Where, then, does athletics fall? The Grants Commission says it will not fund athletics because the Committee exists to fund academic units. The Provincial Sport Governing Body, the Ministry of Sports says, university sports is an education prerogative. I find myself extremely frustrated because I don't know who is supposed to fund us. Perhaps you can shed some light on this?

Ms. Abby Hoffman: I don't know if I can shed any light on the solution. I might be able to shed some light on the problem. Let me just ask whether there is anyone here from the Provincial Government of Ontario whom I understand is one of the funders. The reason I touched briefly on the issue of jurisdictions was simply to say this -- that in the context of the sport system and organizing the jurisdiction of the traditional sport governing bodies, it is quite clear which level is responsible for which type of sport. Insofar as the funding arrangements are concerned, while the total absolute amount might not be sufficient, "who" is responsible has been addressed I think to most people's satisfaction. But, when it comes to university sport, there are two barriers to resolution. One, is the problem you have alluded to that at the provincial government level, the ministries responsible for sport are not the same as the ministries responsible for advancement of education. But the second problem, one that needs to be addressed, is what level of the sport system is it that university sport is serving? If it is high performance sport, then there is no question about the requirements for our financial involvement at the federal level. If it is domestic sport, and that is why a decision of how we define high performance sport is a very critical one, if the main thrust of the university is in domestic sport, then as far as the federal government is concerned, we would be providing money for coordination, organizational management, infrastructure, and program development, but not program delivery. Program delivery in a domestic sport domain is a provincial responsibility. The difficulty is that there isn't an absolutely clear statement about how much of what the university sport scene is doing has to do with high performance sport and how much of it has to do with what may loosely be called domestic sport.

Dr. John Dewar: I would like to respond to that last comment. I feel I can speak for the University of Saskatchewan. We have attempted to carry on a dialogue for quite a number of years with the provincial government both through advanced education and through the Department of Health and Recreation concerning some means of getting access to funding for university sport. And as Joyce Fromson has said, it is happening in Manitoba. You get pitched back and forth like a ping pong ball and there has been no answer forthcoming concerning funding. The dilemma is there, and how we approach it is superfluous. It is even worse than that. Our Deputy Minister of Culture and Recreation has openly advocated construction of a field house downtown in the city of Regina instead of at the university. Not only is he not positive, he is negative.

Dr. Bob Steadward: We have achieved some success in Alberta through the formation of an Alberta University Athletic Association which is being received with openmindedness by the Sport Council and the Department for Advanced Education. There seems to be a legitimate intent on the part of the Alberta Provincial Government to recognize that University sport is unique in that it does attempt to service both, via Sport Canada, domestic and high performance athletes. We feel that there is some glimmer of hope, that there is going to be a legitimate effort made to provide additional funding to university athletics because it is quite different from the rest of the sporting system. Maybe it's just a case of banging your head against the wall a sufficient number of times and finally they'll notice you.

Unidentified Speaker: I would like to address my question to Mary Keyes, and also perhaps to Stu Robbins. Dr. Keye's comment's were relative to the CIAU. It was suggested to the people here that they should reread the minutes of the CIAU session. I think it is something like 23 of 47 or 48 institutions in the country which have an integrated relationship between Physical Education and Athletics as an administrative unit. When I read the calendars of many of those 23 (and 2 of the representatives of these institutions are on the stage), they have the title of Director of Physical Education and Athletics and yet they send someone else to the CIAU. Then when they have the opportunity to reread the CIAU minutes, they are not necessarily happy with what they read. Why do you not take a stronger role in the CIAU relative to some of these issues and attendance?

Dr. Mary Keyes: A few years ago, my President said to me that I should go to the CIAU meetings and take the two votes. I really believe that in our institution we have two chairmen -- the chair of women's athletics and the chair of men's athletics -- and they have the responsibility to represent our institution. However, we have a policy in our institution that when issues are coming up and after they have been discussed, that we meet in the School with our Vice-President and our President and with our President of the Committee on Athletics. I don't see anything in the CIAU minutes to suggest that they aren't taking the views of our institution there. I can afford to send a third person to CIAU meetings and I did. Last year we held the CCUPEA meetings at the same site so that we would have Deans and Directors at the CIAU meetings; I think that's important. I think we should have the Presidents there too, as someone suggested this morning. I think the more observers we can get, the more people who understand the complexities of the issues in athletics, the more involved we can get on our own campus about the complexities, the better decisions we are going to make.

Dr. Stu Robbins: It is only recently that we have come to realize the importance of input into things such as the CIAU and the OUAA and OWIAA. I think it is not quite true to suggest that we haven't been involved. The last couple of years we have been, but it was a matter of time.

Dr. Mary Keyes: That's also what I was saying. I think it should be something more than an observer role. Even though you have a particular institutional position when you go, surely, a dialogue takes place and feedback from around the country will have an impact on the decisions. In fact, you may change the particular position you started with on some issues. However, if you examine some of the voting procedures, you will see that there has been a split vote from many institutions on a number of issues, and that might stop.

Dr. Stu Robbins: I agree.

Mr. Dave Copp: I would like to go back to the comments made in regard to the financing of interuniversity athletics and the quest for funds from other sources. I think that some of us have never seen anyone else responsible for the funding of intercollegiate athletics other than the students in our own institutions. I think we have been under the false expectations that intercollegiate athletics exist because the students want to compete amongst themselves. It is fairly evident if you are in the capacity that I'm in that students are forever coming in the door to request a new intercollegiate team of some sort or other when they could compete locally. There are all kinds of competitions locally, but the students want to go down the road and meet and compete against other university students. So if you have that mental set, when you think of financing, you don't think of going outside the university for funding to help your program. Now if you do decide to go outside the university to fund your regular program, then you must be prepared to consider there may be other objectives that have to be reached. If the money comes from municipalities, or it comes from the province, they have objectives and they may not always be in concert with what we have traditionally done in intercollegiate athletics. So I often think that we go seeking this money as a short term solution without thinking about what the long term implications are. I think that's probably where most of us have to give a lot of thought. Do we want to go that way, and what kinds of hooks would the province put on their contribution and can we meet that kind of a mandate?

Dr. Stu Robbins: Rather than focus on the actual funding issue which Henry Janzen will do later, perhaps we could address the kinds of limits that come with external funding.

Unidentified Speaker: Miss Hoffman, this morning you spoke about the idea of governments working in relation with the universities and providing things like training centres, without disrupting the existing programs which are already in place. I would like to comment on the fact that training centres do create inequities within the system. They create imbalances in competition and in such things like that. I guess the first example that comes to mind is perhaps York. They were designated the training centre for gymnastics and they have dominated the OUAA for the past several years. Would you like to comment on this?

Ms Abby Hoffman: Well, you might have picked a better example of an imbalance being as a result of a training centre. For all practical purposes, as far as Sport Canada is concerned, there is, in fact, no centre in men's gymnastics at York yet. What you have at York and why it will likely become the training centre is the traditional area of strength. I think one of the principles of training centres that should be underscored here is that by and large, (and again it has got to do with the amount of resources that are available for sport in Canada at this time), training centres are a mechanism to consolidate and make existing strong areas more beneficial in particular sports. So what training centers have done in effect is to demonstrate the rich get richer syndrome, in most cases. In some cases the training centre has gone to an institution or location because it has a unique facility. But in most cases, among the criteria that the sport governing body and Sport

Canada use to select the centre are: how many coaches are already there? how many carded athletes are already there? how accessible is the institution as a venue to competition? what are the sport medical and sport science services and resources like? So all I am saying is that the imbalances that already exist in many sports in Canada may be hiked by a training centre. But those are imbalances which have existed for some time in a great many cases. So again, I made the caution this morning about immediately assuming that the 16 centres in CIAU sports are in and of themselves going to disrupt or be the straw that breaks the camel's back in terms of inequity and inappropriateness of competition among institutions.

Dr. Henry Janzen: I would like to address my question to Abby Hoffman. I represent an institution that believes that there are common goals with Sport Canada and that there are some things that we could work on together. Very specifically, certainly the fitness testing and practical research area is obvious. But, there are other areas that are also very obvious -- the travel subsidy, and the appointment of coaches. Working together, for example with dual appointments, makes me nervous when I find it almost impossible to get a long term commitment. And, certainly right now, even though the travel subsidy has been with us for a long time, I think there are many athletic directors in this room who are nervous. Will it continue? And so the concern that I have is that at times there is a good feeling, there is a move from the institutional point of view to share and work together with Sport Canada, but the feeling though is that there is only soft support. And soft support comes because there isn't a long-term commitment. I think that is one of our real concerns when I look to the future in terms of development of programs.

Ms. Abby Hoffman: Well, I can't pass judgement on some of your perceptions because they are perceptions and stand as that. What I can say though, is that long term commitments can most readily be not only made but maintained where they fit the jurisidictional responsibilities of the parties making the commitment. The problem is that Sport Canada got into centres and supported centres that for whatever reasons did not include athletes of the level for which Sport Canada has a primary responsibility. Also, where there are cost cutting measures to be undertaken. Those programs that have least fit into the jurisdiction of the responsibilities of any agency, your institutions, are going to be the most vulnerable. Where do you, when you have budget problems, look to meet your program commitments within your budget ceilings? Understand what I am saying is that the question of long term commitments, is the whole purpose of all this major planning activity we are doing with national sport bodies now to identify things that could be done, it must be clear at the outset that you are buying in and the sport is buying in the things that are within their responsibility area.

Dr. Robert Morford: I would like to address a question to Roger Jackson. Roger, the University of Calgary has gone on record as saying that is is interested in the pursuit of excellence and high performance and I think your records certainly indicate that over the years you have made an effort to hire quality coaches, and run a high profile program. When people hear this, oft times they feel that this is automatically going to be associated with academic abuses. I have not heard this from Calgary at all, and I am wondering what you do at Calgary in order to maintain both proficiency, not only in athletics but also in academics. Is it automatic that once a school makes a commitment to high performance there are going to be academic abuses or can there be a hand in glove high performance in both athletics and acadmics?

Dr. Roger Jackson: I think our aspirations at Calgary are to do the very best that we can within the resources that we have. We have success in two or three sports on a national level, at a very high level. We have about 18 or 19 sports and many of them are, in fact, not ranked in the top ten. But I can easily say that we are really not pushing or are at least not as effective in all of our sport activities as we might be. The key to a great degree is the quality of coaching and the quality of the facilities and time available to groups to use the facilities. We would like to improve the quality of our programming when we move into the new building. We move, for example from 3 gymnasiums to 9 gymnasium areas, so you can see that there is an immediate improvement for volleyball teams and gymnastics teams and everybody else who is competing for the same area. University sport in my opinion is not a win at all cost type of situation. I am very comfortable with people fulfilling full academic requirements and I think we give them the very best possible program we can from the time limitations, financial limitations, and the academic requirements of the university. We have lots of other opportunities outside of the university if people want to be world class athletes, and pursue that particular goal and I think we can live very comfortably with that.

Dr. Stu Robbins: Thank you very much indeed, Mary Keyes, Roger Jackson, Abby Hoffman. This is a topic with which each of our universities must deal. I think it challenges us to clarify our philosophy to define our objectives so that we can boycott some of these external agencies without losing everything in which we believe.

SECTION 4. INTERNAL FACTORS AFFECTING INTERUNIVERSITY ATHLETICS

- INTERNAL FACTORS AFFECTING ELITE SPORT IN CANADIAN UNIVERSITIES
  -- D.M. SEMOTIUK

- PROBLEM AREAS FOR INTERUNIVERSITY ATHLETICS FROM A REGISTRAR'S
  POINT OF VIEW -- E.A. CHARD

- TOWARD EQUIVALENCE OF OPPORTUNITY -- M. POMFRET

INTERNAL FACTORS AFFECTING ELITE SPORT IN
CANADIAN UNIVERSITIES

D.M. SEMOTIUK

It should be recognized that sport, high level sport, is an important social institution in Canadian culture -- although some would challenge its overall importance and significance. The bottom line is that sport impacts on the lives of all Canadians.

Within this context, it is assumed that Canadian universities must be committed to playing a role in extending sport participation and development opportunities to their students. This is achieved through the offering of basic instruction, recreational and intramural sport opportunities, and interuniversity sport opportunities. These programs must be in harmony and entirely consistent with the aims of higher education. Canadian universities have expressed the view that their support of interuniversity athletics can be rationalized by the fact that the experience represents an enrichment of the educational process.

It is my contention that Canadian interuniversity athletics has evolved largely in response to the demands and needs placed before it by reacting, rather than initiating. The watchwords seem to be maintenance, status quo and fire-fighting. Planning initiatives and activities have occurred, but these have tended to be carried out in isolation. Indeed, there is considerable support for the contention that reactive and piecemeal responses are a reflex of the nature of Canadian interuniversity athletics. There appears to be an urgent need for Canadian interuniversity sport to develop more momentum than it has generated to this point. By consolidating existing information and experiences, bold new proposals can be enthusiastically introduced. All the participants must reach agreement on the role they are to play within the system and formal and informal communication models must be developed to ensure that greater co-ordination exists amongst all the system's players.

Within the context of the conference structure and the imposed time limits, this presentation focuses on selected internal factors affecting elite sport in Canadian universities. Questions are posed, debate is encouraged and stimulated, and solutions offered. The following areas are examined: a philosophy of interuniversity sport; operative goals of interuniversity sport and internal issues, including, scope of program offerings, evaluation/ assessment/resource allocation, corporate sponsorship/media relations, marketing strategies and plans, and liability coverage.

TABLE 1. VERTICAL AND HORIZONTAL ORGANIZATION MATRIX:
UNIVERSITIES AND INTERUNIVERSITY SPORT

LEVEL	UNIVERSITY STRUCTURES	BRIDGING THE GAP STRUCTURES	INTERUNIVERSITY SPORT STRUCTURES
INSTITUTIONAL	UNIVERSITY OF WESTERN ONTARIO (UWO)		UNIVERSITY OF WESTERN ONTARIO UWO
REGIONAL	COUNCIL OF ONTARIO UNIVERSITIES (COU)	ONTARIO COMMISSION ON INTERUNIVERSITY ATHLETICS* (OCIA)	ONTARIO UNIVERSITIES ATHLETIC ASSOCIATION (OUAA) ONTARIO WOMEN'S INTERUNIVERSITY ATHLETIC ASSOCIATION (OWIAA)
NATIONAL	ASSOCIATION OF UNIVERSITIES AND COLLEGES OF CANADA (AUCC)		CANADIAN INTERUNIVERSITY ATHLETIC UNION (CIAU)
INTERNATIONAL	ASSOCIATION OF COMMONWEALTH UNIVERSITIES (ACU) INTERNATIONAL ASSOCIATION OF UNIVERSITIES (ICU)		FEDERATION DU SPORTS INTERNATIONAL UNIVERSITAIRES (FISU)

* BEGAN OPERATION IN SEPTEMBER, 1985.

University Organizations and their Interuniversity Athletics Structures

The organizations for universities and interuniversity sport are identified in Table 1. The data suggest the presence of a vertical structure which appears to serve the needs of both the universities and interuniversity sport well -- from the institutional level to the international level. With few exceptions, formal structures whose primary purpose would be to bridge the gap between university organizations and their interuniversity sport counterparts have not yet evolved. The recently created Ontario Commission on Interuniversity Athletics is one such exception.

A Philosophy of Interuniversity Athletics

It is essential that individual institutions develop a clear statement on the role that interuniversity athletics is to play within their own university. This process begins by considering the University's Mission Statement. The example of the University of Western Ontario is offered in Table 2. The approach that the University takes with its interuniversity sport program must be consistent with its Mission statement. The linkage between the two must be well established, dependable, and accountable.

Recent discussions in Ontario surrounding the matter of intercollegiate athletic conference realignment have provided the stimulus for Ontario universities to develop, or to up-date, their institution's philosophy of

TABLE 2. THE UNIVERSITY OF WESTERN ONTARIO MISSION STATEMENT
(APPROVED BY SENATE - DECEMBER 8, 1983, APPROVED BY
BOARD OF GOVERNORS - JANUARY 26, 1984)

THE UNIVERSITY OF WESTERN ONTARIO IS A CENTRE OF LEARNING. ITS' PURPOSE IS TO BE OF BENEFIT TO SOCIETY THROUGH THE PURSUIT AND PRESERVATION OF KNOWLEDGE AND THE PROVISION OF AN ENVIRONMENT WITHIN WHICH STUDENTS MAY ACQUIRE THE CRITICAL UNDERSTANDING, HUMANE VALUES, AND SKILLS NECESSARY TO APPLY THIS KNOWLEDGE EFFECTIVELY.

PURSUIT AND PRESERVATION OF KNOWLEDGE

TEACHING AND LEARNING

THE UNIVERSITY'S CONTRIBUTION TO THE COMMUNITY

---

interuniversity athletics. The Report of the Special Committee on Intercollegiate Athletics (1985) offered the following recommendations:

> ". . . . that each university develop a statement of philosophy on interuniversity athletics, embodying certain defined principles, and have this statement formally approved by its' senate and board (or governing council) by the end of the 1985-86 academic year. . . . . that each university then take immediate steps to make this philosophy effective both on its' own campus and its' involvement in the athletic leagues." (p. i)

TABLE 3. SENATE PRINCIPLES GOVERNING INTERUNIVERSITY ATHLETICS: THE UNIVERSITY OF WESTERN ONTARIO, LONDON, ONTARIO (APPROVED MAY, 1984.)

PRINCIPLE #1
IN EACH UNIVERSITY, THE ACADEMIC AUTHORITIES SHOULD CONTROL ATHLETICS.

PRINCIPLE #2
THE MEMBER INSTITUTIONS SHOULD BE COMMITTED TO OFFERING SPORTS PROGRAMS OF EXCELLENCE THAT FUNCTION WITHIN THE PHILOSOPHICAL FRAMEWORK OF AN EDUCATIONAL ENVIRONMENT.

PRINCIPLE #3
THE MEMBER INSTITUTIONS SHOULD PROVIDE EQUAL OPPORTUNITIES IN ATHLETICS FOR MEN AND WOMEN.

PRINCIPLE #4
THE MEMBER INSTITUTIONS SHOULD FOSTER INTRA-CONFERENCE COMPETITION INVOLVING A WIDE RANGE OF ACTIVITIES.

PRINCIPLE #5
THE MEMBER INSTITUTIONS SHOULD NOT OFFER FIRST PARTY ATHLETIC SCHOLARSHIPS.

PRINCIPLE #6
THE MEMBER INSTITUTIONS SHOULD ADHERE TO THE PRINCIPLE THAT THE STUDENT-ATHLETE SHOULD BE HELD ACCOUNTABLE TO THE SAME ACADEMIC STANDARDS AS OTHER STUDENTS AND SHOULD BE MAKING PROGRESS TOWARDS THE COMPLETION OF AN ACADEMIC PROGRAM.

PRINCIPLE #7
AN AGREED UPON EXTERNAL MONITORING SYSTEM OF PLAYER ELIGIBILITY PRACTICES SHOULD BE ACCEPTED BY ALL MEMBERS.

The development of a statement of philosophy should involve broad participation on the part of those who are either directly or indirectly associated
with athletics. Student-athletes, coaches, academic faculty, athletic administrators, central administration, alumni, and representatives from the community should be provided with the opportunity to furnish input along the way.
The University of Western Ontario's Senate Principles Governing Interuniversity Athletics statement is an example of what the finished product might look
like (see Table 3).

Once the internal process has concluded, and the statement has been
agreed upon, it is necessary to have the position considered at the league or
association level. If one were to accept the assumption that athletic conferences bring together like-minded institutions, then it is imperative that
there be concurrence among those institutions that make up the league structure. It is obvious that differing views exist on the acceptance of this
assumption.

Institutions must be able to pass judgement on the compatibility of their
philosophical position with the associations and organizations they have
affiliation with or membership in. In most instances, some degree of flexibility must be applied. Three examples which show the external application of
a philosophical position are presented: The Council of Ontario Universities
Principles Underlying a Statement of Philosophy on Interuniversity Athletics
(Table 4); Ontario Women's Interuniversity Athletic Association: Philosophic

TABLE 4. COUNCIL OF ONTARIO UNIVERSITIES PRINCIPLES UNDERLYING
A STATEMENT OF PHILOSOPHY ON INTERUNIVERSITY ATHLETICS (1985)

PRINCIPLE #1
IN THE UNIVERSITY, ACADEMIC AUTHORITIES SHOULD EXERCISE RESPONSIBILITY
OVER THE ATHLETICS POLICY.

PRINCIPLE #2
THE SAME ACADEMIC STANDARDS SHOULD APPLY TO ALL STUDENTS.

PRINCIPLE #3
THERE SHOULD BE EQUAL OPPORTUNITY IN INTER-UNIVERSITY ATHLETICS FOR MEN
AND WOMEN.

PRINCIPLE #4
PARTICIPATION IN INTERUNIVERSITY ATHLETICS SHOULD INVOLVE A COMMITMENT BY
THE INSTITUTION TO THE PROGRAMME.

PRINCIPLE #5
NO INSTITUTION SHOULD OFFER FIRST PARTY ATHLETIC AWARDS.

Statement (Table 5); and The Canadian Interuniversity Athletic Union Constitutional Objectives (Table 6).

Operative Goals of Interuniversity Athletics

A recent study conducted by Chelladurai and Danylchuk (1984) examined the
perceptions of the operative goals of intercollegiate athletics. Ninety
intercollegiate athletic administrators from across Canada participated in the
study. The operative goals included in the study were 1) Entertainment, 2)
National Sport Development, 3) Financial, 4) Transmission of Culture, 5)
Career Opportunities, 6) Public Relations, 7) Athlete's Personal Growth,
8) Prestige, and 9) Achieved Excellence (Table 7). The rankings of these
nine objectives were analyzed on the basis of the sex of the respondents, size
of the university, and the conference membership. In addition, the relationship between respondents' ratings of these objectives, and their attitudes
toward athletic scholarships, recruitment practices, and eligibility were also
examined. The results showed that the various subgroups of athletic administrators were relatively homogeneous in ranking Transmission of Culture,
Athlete's Personal Growth, Public Relations, and Prestige as the most important set of operative goals. As expected, it was found that the administrators
from the non-central region (Maritime and Western Provinces) were more in
favour of athletic scholarships than the administrators from the central

TABLE 5. ONTARIO WOMEN'S INTERUNIVERSITY ATHLETIC ASSOCIATION
PHILOSOPHY STATEMENT (1985)

PRINCIPLE #1
THE O.W.I.A.A. IS COMMITTED TO THE PROVISION OF QUALITY INTERUNIVERSITY
SPORT COMPETITION FOR FEMALE STUDENT-ATHLETES WITHIN THE EDUCATIONAL
ENVIRONMENT OF THE UNIVERSITIES.

PRINCIPLE #2
THE O.W.I.A.A. IS COMMITTED TO THE TRAINING AND INVOLVEMENT OF WOMEN AS
LEADERS IN SPORT. IT OFFERS ROLE MODELS FOR WOMEN IN SPORT, LEADERSHIP
TRAINING FOR WOMEN IN VARIOUS ADMINISTRATIVE CAPACITIES WITHIN
INTERUNIVERSITY ATHLETICS, AS WELL AS PROVISION OF LEADERSHIP TO OTHER
SPORT GROUPS.

PRINCIPLE #3
THE O.W.I.A.A. IS COMMITTED TO THE BELIEF THAT SPORT MAY ENHANCE THE
INTRINSIC VALUES OF SPORTSMANSHIP, FAIRPLAY, DISCIPLINE, SELF-MOTIVATION,
COOPERATION, AND INTEGRITY, ALL OF WHICH ARE BENEFICIAL TO THE INDIVIDUAL
THROUGHOUT HER LIFE.

TABLE 6. C.I.A.U. CONSTITUTIONAL OBJECTIVES (1985)

WHEREAS A UNIVERSITY ATHLETIC PROGRAM MUST IN FACT AS WELL AS IN THEORY NEVER LOSE SIGHT OF VALUES THAT ARE BASIC TO A SOUND EDUCATIONAL PROGRAM, BE IT RESOLVED THAT THE FOLLOWING GUIDELINES EXPRESS THE INTENT OF THE C.I.A.U. CONSTITUTIONAL OBJECTIVES:

1. TO PROVIDE ALL MEMBERS WITH A MEDIUM FOR DISCUSSION OF PROBLEMS OF COMMON INTEREST.

2. TO ENCOURAGE AND/OR CO-ORDINATE INTER-ASSOCIATION COMPETITION AND NATIONAL CHAMPIONSHIPS AND TO DEVELOP INTERNATIONAL COMPETITION.

3. TO ENCOURAGE, REFLECT AND INTERPRET TO THE CANADIAN PUBLIC THE HIGHEST POSSIBLE STANDARD OF EXCELLENCE IN SPORT IN AN EDUCATIONAL CONTEXT.

4. TO ENCOURAGE, REFLECT AND INTERPRET TO THE CANADIAN PUBLIC THE ACHIEVEMENT OF EXCELLENCE THROUGH THE HIGHEST POSSIBLE ETHICAL STANDARDS OF SPORTSMANSHIP.

5. TO PUBLISH AND DISSEMINATE INFORMATION CONCERNING ASSOCIATION, NATIONAL AND INTERNATIONAL INTERUNIVERSITY ATHLETIC ACTIVITY.

6. TO ENTER INTO AGREEMENT WITH OTHER SPORT BODIES, AND GOVERNMENT AGENCIES, IN CASES WHERE IT MAY BE DEEMED DESIRABLE.

7. TO ENCOURAGE ITS MEMBERS TO PROVIDE LEADERSHIP IN THE DEVELOPMENT OF SPORT IN THE COMMUNITY.

8. TO SET ELIGIBILITY REGULATIONS UNDER WHICH ALL UNION AND ASSOCIATION COMPETITIONS LEADING TO UNION CHAMPIONSHIPS ARE CONDUCTED.

9. TO APPROVE SUCH PLAYING RULES AND CODES AS MAY BE DEEMED SUITABLE TO GOVERN INTERUNIVERSITY SPORT WHILE TAKING INTO CONSIDERATION THE RULES AND REGULATIONS OF OTHER SPORT GOVERNING BODIES.

10. TO DEVELOP FUND RAISING MECHANISMS TO SUPPORT THE ACTIVITIES OF THE UNION.

11. TO EXERCISE SUCH POWERS AND RESPONSIBILITIES AS MAY BE VESTED IN THE UNION BY THE MEMBERS FROM TIME TO TIME.

---

region (Ontario and Quebec). Also, higher ratings of Public Relations, Prestige, Entertainment, and Financial Objectives were associated with stronger support for athletic scholarships and unrestrained recruitment. It was noted that administrator's goal orientation, while congruent with those students from selected universities, were contrary to the prescriptions and proscriptons of prominent educators.

It is important that operative goals of interuniversity athletics be priorized at the institutional level and that these goals reflect a consensus view shared by the academic community, the administration of the university, and its athletic program. These goals will probably differ from institution to institution. It goes, without saying, that institutional policies, procedures, and programs that are encouraged should accurately reflect the statement of philosophy and the priorized operative goals.

TABLE 7. SCALE OF ATHLETIC PRIORITIES (SAP)
(Chelladurai and Danylchuk, 1984)

---

1. ENTERTAINMENT - TO PROVIDE A SOURCE OF ENTERTAINMENT FOR THE STUDENT BODY, FACULTY/STAFF, ALUMNI AND COMMUNITY.

2. NATIONAL SPORT DEVELOPMENT - TO CONTRIBUTE TO THE NATIONAL SPORT DEVELOPMENT.

3. FINANCIAL - TO GENERATE REVENUE FOR THE UNIVERSITY.

4. TRANSMISSION OF CULTURE - TO TRANSMIT THE CULTURE AND TRADITION OF THE UNIVERSITY AND SOCIETY.

5. CAREER OPPORTUNITIES - TO PROVIDE THOSE ATHLETIC EXPERIENCES THAT WILL INCREASE CAREER OPPORTUNITIES FOR THE ATHLETES.

6. PUBLIC RELATIONS - TO ENHANCE THE UNIVERSITY-COMMUNITY RELATIONS.

7. ATHLETE'S PERSONAL GROWTH - TO PROMOTE THE ATHLETE'S PERSONAL GROWTH AND HELATH (PHYSICAL, MENTAL, AND EMOTIONAL).

8. PRESTIGE - TO ENHANCE THE PRESTIGE OF THE UNIVERSITY, STUDENTS, FACULTY/-STAFF, ALUMNI AND COMMUNITY.

9. ACHIEVED EXCELLENCE - TO SUPPORT THOSE ATHLETES PERFORMING AT A HIGH LEVEL OF EXCELLENCE (RELATIVE TO ATHLETES IN OTHER UNIVERSITIES).

Scope of Programs

In this climate of economic uncertainty and budgetary restraint, the matter of scope of interuniversity sport program offerings receives increased attention. In this regard, institutions face the difficult task of having to make decisions on program reduction and priorized resource allocation.

A recent survey conducted in the United States has identified some interesting trends in the area of institution sponsored sports programs. Data for 1981 and 1984 were taken from the men's and women's editions of the Directory of College Athletics,(1985) published by Ray Franks Publishing Co.

Table 8 offers a glimpse at how sports programs have evolved in the United States since 1981, comparing the number of programs offered in each sport for men and women; the percentage of schools sponsoring each sport; the increase or reduction in each sport since 1981; the total number of sports programs for men and women; and the total number of institutions sponsoring some form of intercollegiate athletics.

Although the number of senior colleges offering men's programs has increased slightly from 1,217 to 1,249, the number of programs offered at those institutions has decreased from 8,806 to 8,502. While the average senior college offered 7.24 men's sport programs in 1981, that number was down to 6.65 in 1984. Increases were detected in basketball, cross-country, and soccer; decreases in wrestling, gymnastics, golf, tennis, track and field, and baseball.

According to the data, women's sports programs still lag behind, although they are beginning to catch up. In all, 1,278 senior college institutions offer women's sports, up from 1,131 in 1981. Those colleges sponsor a total of 6,883 programs or 5.35 per school, an increase of 543 programs over 1981's 6,290. The average per institution is down from the 5.56 offered in 1981. The most notable increases in women's sport programs occurred in cross-country, softball, soccer, basketball, and volleyball; decreases were found in gymnastics, field hockey, and golf.

Table 9 provides an indication of institutional participation in CIAU activities for the 1985-86 academic year. Of the forty-five (45) members of the CIAU, eight (8) institutions offer a full CIAU program for their students - McMAster, Queens, Toronto, Western Ontario, York, Alberta, British Colombia and Calgary. Twelve (12) institutions offer six (6) or less activities - U.P.E.I., St-Thomas, Bishop's, Concordia, Montreal, Chicoutimi, Trois-Rivieres, Trent, Brandon, Lakehead, Regina, and Winnipeg. Men's and women's gymnastics has the least number of CIAU member institution involvement with ten (10) participants. Based on these data, a thought-provoking report submitted to the CIAU Task Force on Competitive Scheduling suggests that future CIAU championship models take into consideration the important factors of competitive balance, university size, and university academic orientation.

TABLE 8. SENIOR COLLEGE SPORTS PARTICIPATION SURVEY

SENIOR COLLEGE INTERCOLLEGIATE ATHLETIC PROGRAMS

	MEN'S PROGRAMS					WOMEN'S PROGRAMS				
	1984	%	1981	%	Diff.	1984	%	1981	%	Diff.
BASKETBALL	1220	95.4	1185	97.4	35	1170	91.5	1080	95.5	90
VOLLEYBALL	Accurate data not available					1018	79.7	930	82.2	88
BASEBALL	955	74.7	991	81.4	-36	3		0		3
SOFTBALL	Accurate data not available					766	60.0	640	56.6	126
TENNIS	938	73.3	980	80.6	-42	935	73.2	912	80.6	23
GOLF	785	61.4	850	70.0	-65	197	15.4	243	21.5	-46
CROSS-COUNTRY	840	65.7	790	65.0	50	613	48.0	430	33.6	183
TRACK	738	57.7	770	63.3	-32	619	48.4	554	49.0	65
SOCCER	762	59.6	660	54.2	102	180	14.1	60	5.3	120
FOOTBALL	657	51.4	665	54.6	-8	0	0	0		0
WRESTLING	388	30.3	485	40.0	-97	0	0	0		0
SWIMMING/DIVING	411	32.1	460	37.8	-49	440	34.4	438	38.7	2
GYMNASTICS	76	5.9	139	11.4	-63	166	13.0	240	21.2	-74
ICE HOCKEY	133	10.3	138	11.3	-5	25	2.0	5		20
FIELD HOCKEY	0	0	1		-1	273	21.4	345	30.5	-72
LA CROSSE	146	11.4	140	11.5	6	123	9.6	115	10.2	8
WATER POLO	55	4.3	70	5.8	-15	4		9		-5
FENCING	74	5.8	100	8.2	-26	71	5.6	89	7.9	-18
SKIING	53	4.1	60	5.0	-7	55	4.3	50	4.4	5
RIFLE	77	6.0	75	6.2	2	15	1.2	2		13
CREW	64	5.0	66	5.4	-2	56	4.4	25	2.2	31
SAILING	34	2.7	40	3.3	-6	13	1.0	4		9
BOWLING	30	2.3	60	4.9	-30	18	1.4	33	3.0	-15
SQUASH	25	2.0	29	2.4	-4	19	1.5	8		11
JUDO/KARATE	17	1.3	32	2.6	-15	3		0		3
RUGBY	12		11		1	1		1		0
BADMINTON	1		3	0	-2	17	1.3	46	4.1	-29
ARCHERY	1		2		-1	7		18	1.6	-11
CYCLING	1		2		-1	1		2		-1
CRICKET	2		1		1	0	0	0		0
RIDING	3		2		1	19	1.5	3		16
RODEO	2		1		1	1		0		1
SYNCH. SWIMMING	0	0	0	0	0	4		7		-3
POLO	2		0	0	2			1		
TOTAL PROGRAMS	8502		8806		-304	6833		6290		543
TOTAL COLLEGES	1279		1217		62	1278		1131		147
AVERAGE PER COLLEGE	6.65		7.24		-.59	5.35		5.56		-.21

TABLE 9. CANADIAN INTERUNIVERSITY ATHLETIC UNION

DECLARATION OF PARTICIPATION SUMMARY

Year 1985-86

	BB M	BB W	CC M	CC W	FH W	FB M	GYM M	GYM W	HOC M	SOC M	S&D M	S&D W	T&F M	T&F W	VB M	VB W	W M	TOTAL
Acadia	x	x			x	x			x	x	x	x	x	x		x		11
Dalhousie	x	x	x	x	x				x	x	x	x	x	x	x	x		13
Memorial		x	x	x	x					x	x	x	x	x	x	x	x	12
Moncton			x	x					x	x			x	x	x	x		8
Mount Allison	x	x			x	x			x	x	x	x	x	x	x		x	12
New Brunswick	x	x	x	x	x				x	x	x	x	x	x	x	x	x	14
U.P.E.I.	x	x			x				x	x						x		6
St. Francis Xavier	x	x			x	x			x	x						x	x	8
St. Mary's	x	x			x	x			x	x			x	x				8
St. Thomas									x				x	x				3
Bishop's	x	x				x				x								4
Concordia	x	x				x			x	x							x	6
Laval	x	x	x	x							x	x	x	x		x		9
McGill	x	x	x	x	x	x			x	x	x	x	x	x	x	x		14
Montreal									x						x			2
Chicoutimi	x												x	x				3
Trois-Rivières			x	x					x	x					x	x		6
Sherbrooke			x	x					x	x	x		x	x	x	x		9

Institution	37	37	29	29	24	23	10	10	35	33	29	29	31	31	30	35	23	
Brock	X	X	X		X				X	X	X	X	X	X	X	X	X	13
Carleton	X	X			X	X			X	X	X	X			X	X	X	8
Guelph	X	X	X	X	X				X		X	X			X	X	X	15
Laurentian	X	X	X	X	X				X	X	X	X	X		X	X	X	12
McMaster	X	X	X	X	X	X	X	X	X	X	X	X	X	X	X	X	X	17 *
Ottawa	X	X	X	X	X	X			X	X		X			X	X		9
Queen's	X	X	X	X	X	X	X	X	X	X	X	X	X	X	X	X	X	17 *
R.M.C.	X	X	X	X					X	X	X	X			X	X	X	10
Ryerson	X	X	X	X					X		X	X	X	X		X	X	8
Toronto	X	X	X	X	X	X	X	X	X	X	X	X	X	X	X	X	X	17 *
Trent	X	X	X						X		X	X			X	X	X	6
Waterloo	X	X	X	X	X	X			X	X	X	X	X	X	X	X	X	16
Western Ontario	X	X	X	X	X	X	X	X	X	X	X	X	X	X	X	X	X	17 *
Wilfrid Laurier	X	X	X		X		X	X	X	X	X	X	X	X	X	X	X	14
Windsor	X	X	X	X	X	X			X	X	X	X	X	X	X		X	13
York	X	X	X	X	X	X	X	X	X	X	X	X	X	X	X	X	X	17 *
Brandon	X	X									X							3
Lakehead	X	X							X		X					X		4
Manitoba	X	X	X		X	X	X	X	X	X	X	X			X	X	X	15
Regina	X	X							X	X					X	X	X	6
Winnipeg	X	X							X	X						X	X	4
Alberta	X	X	X	X	X	X	X	X	X	X	X	X	X	X	X	X	X	17 *
British Columbia	X	X	X	X	X	X	X	X	X	X	X	X	X	X	X	X	X	17 *
Calgary	X	X	X	X	X	X	X	X	X	X	X	X	X	X	X	X	X	17 *
Lethbridge	X	X	X	X					X	X	X	X			X	X		10
Saskatchewan	X	X	X	X	X				X	X	X	X	X	X	X		X	13
Victoria	X	X	X	X	X				X	X	X	X	X	X	X	X	X	12
TOTAL	37	37	29	29	24	23	10	10	35	33	29	29	31	31	30	35	23	

45 CIAU MEMBERS   * FULL CIAU PROGRAM

71

Evaluation/Sports Assessment/Resource Allocation

Few would dispute the fact that less flexibility exists within athletic program budgets of today. Clearly, it is quite apparent that this reality must be addressed through sound planning and rational decision making. Decisions on program reduction and resource allocation require objectivity. University athletic programs must utilize proper evaluation procedures to ascertain cost-benefit ratios for all programs currently being offered. The assessment of program needs, the determination of program funding priorities, and program rationalization will occupy the time of athletic administrators

TABLE 10. MCGILL UNIVERSITY
DEPARTMENT OF ATHLETICS
SPORT CLASSIFICATION SYSTEM

THE SPORTS CLASSIFICATION SYSTEM HAS BEEN PUT INTO EFFECT BY THE ATHLETICS BOARD TO OBJECTIFY DECISION-MAKING AS IT RELATES TO THE ALLOCATION OF RESOURCES FOR INTERCOLLEGIATE ATHLETICS.

CRITERIA

1.	COMPETITIVE STRUCTURE	20 POINTS
2.	COACHING EXCELLENCE	14 POINTS
3.	FACILITIES AND EQUIPMENT	13 POINTS
4.	PARTICIPANT DEMAND AND POPULARITY	8 POINTS
5.	FEEDER SYSTEM AND RECRUITING POTENTIAL	7 POINTS
6.	DURATION AND SEASON OF ACTIVITY	6 POINTS
7.	COMPETITIVE SUCCESS	6 POINTS
8.	TRAINING COMMITTMENT	6 POINTS
9.	UNIT COST OF ACTIVITY	6 POINTS
10.	POTENTIAL REVENUE	5 POINTS
11.	PUBLIC RELATIONS VALUE	5 POINTS
12.	TRADITION	4 POINTS

TOTAL RATING 100 POINTS

during the latter half of this decade. Two approaches that have been utilized in dealing with this issue are: McGill University's Sport Classification System (Table 10) and the University of Western Ontario's Sport Assessment Procedure (Table 11).

Corporate Sponsorship

During the next decade, Canadian interuniversity athletic programs will be forced to develop innovative approaches to improve current operating budgets. In addition to expanding upon existing revenue generating programs, i.e., gate receipts, summer sport camps, special projects etc., intercollegiate athletic departments will have

TABLE 11. UNIVERSITY OF WESTERN ONTARIO
INTERCOLLEGIATE ATHLETIC PROGRAM
SPORTS ASSESSMENT

EFFECTIVENESS CRITERIA	RATING (1-10) x	WEIGHTING =	TOTAL
1. COACHING COMPETENCE		7	
2. PERFORMANCE LEVEL		6	
3. EXTENT OF COMPETITION		5	
4. SUPPLY OF ATHLETES		4	
5. QUALITY OF FACILITIES		3	
6. QUALITY OF TRAINING		2	
7. SPECTATOR APPEAL		1	

to develop strategies which will allow them to access corporate sector funding. It is in this area that potential problems and conflicts will arise. For example, institutions will have to determine the acceptability or non-acceptability of corporate sponsors, i.e., breweries, distilleries, tobacco companies, etc. Institutional and association policies and guidelines should be in place in order to facilitate the decision-making process. Also, further thought will have to be given as to how the corporate sponsorship initiatives of intercollegiate athletic program can be integrated into the University's general fund-raising program. All this must be undertaken at time when the corporate sector has been innundated with a marked increase in requests for financial contributions.

Marketing Strategies and Plans

With few exceptions, most Canadian interuniversity athletic programs have done a poor job in marketing their products both on and off the campus. The athletic programs of the future will have to recognize this as both a need and a potential growth area. As most Canadian universities are fortunate enough to have commerce/business administration academic units on campus, the on-campus expertise is readily available to assist in this area. The message of academic excellence and athletic excellence can be effectively marketed by Canadian universities. Marketing surveys involving the student population, the faculty/staff, the alumni, the general public, the corporate sector, and the media will provide data from which a comprehensive marketing strategy and plan can emerge. Awareness and image can no longer be ignored -- a professional approach is required. Indeed, it is possible to achieve positive results without a major financial outlay.

Liability Insurance Coverage

One of the more immediate threats to present programs is the escalating cost of premiums for liability insurance. Some institutions are finding that insurance companies are no longer willing to renew liability policies at the previous rates. The high in-court and out-of-court settlements that have been granted have hit the insurance industry hard over the last few years, the result being that a few companies are no longer willing to take the risk. Consider the following example of a 15 year old gymnast from New York who fell from the parallel bars during a high school practice and crushed her spinal vertebrae. A $17 million out of court settlement was granted, as the young lady's attorney successfully argued that there was no five-inch thick pad beneath the bars, and that no spotter was there to break her fall.

This matter has become an issue of concern at all levels of government. The Minister of Fitness and Amateur Sport has recently struck a committee to review the matter of liability insurance as it relates to the activities of national sports organizations. Similar initiatives have also been taken by several provincial governments. At this juncture, several options appear to be available:

1. Institutions can continue to keep their programs going without liability coverage.

2. Institutions can cancel their programs.

3. Institutions can continue to offer programs with liability coverage at the higher rates -- it is predictable that program reduction would have to take place in order to meet the higher premium payments that will be required.

4. Institutions, either individually or collectively, can form a self-insurance pool to handle liability claims.

5. Governments may wish to intervene by placing a ceiling on the awards made in liability suits.

Given these recent developments, liability is an issue that must receive serious attention by athletic and university administrators alike. Every effort should be made to ensure that athletic program coaches and staff are made fully aware of the policies and procedures which govern their activities. As a preventative measure, careful, conscientious monitoring and supervision of all program personnel should become a high priority for athletic administrators.

The Environment for Interuniversity Athletics

Ultimately, it is the individual university and its' employees that must be responsible and accountable for the interuniversity athletics program. The policies, procedures, and structures must be founded on the institution's statement on the role of interuniversity athletics -- it is an expression of the beliefs and convictions of that university. The program must be consistent with the academic mission of the university and that reality should never be placed in jeopardy, or for that matter questioned -- the welfare of the student-athlete should never be threatened. It is the student, in the term student-athlete, that should be emphasized. It is within this framework that a healthy, stimulating environment for interuniversity athletics can be created. Reasonable schedules and travel demands will respect the primary reasons that a student attends university -- his/her interest lies in the pursuit of an academic program culminating in a university degree. This should not, and cannot, be interpreted in any other way.

The prevailing attitude and environment that we are striving to create can be best described by the following two terms: excellence and class. Universities should be committed to offering interuniversity athletic programs within the philosophical framework of an educational environment -- these are programs that aspire to the highest standards of individual and collective excellence, and they are to be pursued in a first class way.

Canadian interuniversity sport is at yet another crossroad in its development. Institutional and organizational leaders must show wisdom, courage and vision in the judgements that must be made on the future of interuniversity athletics. A talented after-dinner speaker concluded his address by noting that, "if you don't stand for something, you will fall for anything."

The time is now upon us for Canadian universities to take a stand -- a stand which will guarantee the protection of the student-athlete and the integrity of the university system and its educational mission.

References

A Mechanism for Assessing Cost-Effectiveness of Intercollegiate Sports at the University of Western Ontario. Unpublished paper prepared by the Intercollegiate Athletic Program, University of Western Ontario, 1980, 10 pages.

Chelladurai, P., Haggerty, T.R., Campbell, L. and Wall, S.A. Factor Analytic Study of Effectiveness Criteria in Intercollegiate Athletics. Canadian Journal of Applied Sport Sciences, 1980, 6(2), pp. 81-86.

Chelladurai, P. and Danylchuk, K.E. Operative Goals of Intercollegiate Athletics: Perceptions of Athletic Administrators. Canadian Journal of Applied Sports Sciences, 9.1, 1984, pp. 33-41.

Government of Canada. Partners in Pursuit of Excellence - A National Policy on Amateur Sport: Ottawa: Minister of Supply and Services Canada, 1979, 24 pages.

Liability Insurance Crisis Threatens Interscholastic Sports. Athletic Director and Coach. Madison, Wisconsin: Magna Publications, Volume 4, No. 3, March 1986, pp. 1-2.

Mathews, A.W. Athletics in Canadian Universities - The Report on the AUCC/CIAU Study of Athletic Programs in Canadian Universities. Ottawa: Association of Universities and Colleges of Canada, 1974, 116 pages.

Ontario Women's Interuniversity Athletic Association. Philosophy. Waterloo: Graphic Services, University of Waterloo, 1985, 37 pages.

Report of the Special Committee on Intercollegiate Athletics Conference Realignment. London: Faculty of Physical Education, March, 1985, 47 pages.

Report of the Special Committee on Intercollegiate Athletics. Toronto: Council of Ontario Universities, April, 1985, 57 pages.

Report of the Special Committee on Physical and Health Education and Athletics
    London: The University of Western Ontario, February, 1971, 55 pages.

Sport Classification System. Unpublished document prepared by the Department
    of Athletics, McGill University, 1985, 7 pages.

The Athletic Buiness Senior College Sports Participation Survey. Athletic
    Business. January, 1985, pp. 20-23.

The University of Western Ontario. Statement of Mission. London: Department
    of Graphic Services, 1984, 8 pages.

PROBLEM AREAS FOR INTERUNIVERSITY ATHLETICS FROM A REGISTRAR'S
POINT OF VIEW

ELIZABETH A. CHARD

An interested observer would probably be amazed at the number of official forms which a Registrar signs weekly in the course of his/her duties - and the number is increasing annually. These include passport applications, Statistics Canada enrolment reports, student loan defer payments, academic transcripts, immigration forms of one kind or another, and, of course, degree/diploma parchments. In addition, many registrars hold provincial Supreme Court appointments as Commissioners of Oaths -- hence another battery of legal forms have to be processed.

If you were to check the 'training' for registrars, you would find it varies -- there is none specifically available. Many have been seconded from faculty ranks, others from administrative positions both within the University and outside. In addition to the fact that there are no specific qualifications required, there are usually few if any established procedures at post-secondary institutions concerning the process by which the validity of documents signed can be verified. At best registrars have developed their own procedures; at worst, they sign, keeping their fingers crossed as to the accuracy of what has been placed in front of them. Probably few have queried the legal implications, both personal and professional, should problems arise. The fact remains that in most cases, no one really cares until there is a problem; then everyone is an instant "expert", offering both advice and criticism. Suddenly the Registrar is entirely to blame.

In carrying out the task of signing forms, none give me more qualms than those on athletic eligibility - whether they be those of Canadian Intercollegiate Athletic Union (C.I.A.U.) or those of the Atlantic Universities Athletic Association (A.U.A.A.). As a result, I have been sounding the alarm and acquainting others with my concern for many years. These facts notwithstanding, I never cease to be amazed at the blase attitude sometimes evident on the part of some of my colleagues whether from ignorance or lack of concern, I am not certain.

Rules Themselves

The eligibility regulations are found in the C.I.A.U.'s Operations Manual. The heart of these is found in Regulation C with it's 12 subsections. (See the Appendix which follows this paper). Many of the examples in this paper will refer to this multi-sectional regulation. Revisions and updates to these are promulgated annually after each Annual Meeting by the C.I.A.U. National Office usually in mid to late summer.

I wonder how many registrars have actually been provided with or indeed have requested an actual copy of this <u>Operations Manual</u> and its accompanying <u>Case Book</u>? I suspect that many of my colleagues rely on the "summary of regulations" promulgated primarily for the use of student-athletes.

In addition, each of the six conferences which comprise the C.I.A.U. have the right to legislate exceptions to C.I.A.U. regulations. These must be of a more stringent nature than those of the Union. Here again, Registrars need copies of the legislation and the updates. My experience suggests that it is not sufficient merely to have these documents, they must be understood. This is no mean feat given the technical language which often intrudes. A further complication is that coaches in particular prefer to interpret the intent of the regulation (often as they perceive it), rather than the actual rule itself. This can be a point of never-ending conflict on a campus.

Forms

The C.I.A.U. Eligibility Form is deceptively simple in format and in the amount of the information requested. Two official signatures are required, namely, that of the Athletic Director and the Registrar; hence there would appear to be dual responsibility. However, the fundamental question to be raised is what does the Registrar's signature mean on these forms? Is it limited to a verification of those data items contained in every student's official file held in the University's Records Office? Or, is it a verification of all data items on the sheet itself? This is the crux of the matter and not a situation unique to the C.I.A.U. forms. Indeed, I frequently raise this same query in the Saint Mary's Senate and standing committee meetings vis-a-vis a faculty advisor's signature on a registration form. Does it mean that the form was seen; that the student was counselled; that the correctness of the data was verified; or all of these?

About six years ago my personal involvement with athletic organizations convinced me to clarify my position and responsibility re: C.I.A.U. forms compared with that of the Director of Athletics at my institution. Hence I devised a contract of responsibilities in which I formally indicated for what I was willing to assume responsibility. Simply stated, this responsibility was a follows. In the case of students registered for the first time at Saint Mary's, that they were officially registered on a full-time basis in a degree or diploma programme. In the case of returning students, that they too were also registered and that they successfully had completed a minimum of 18 semester hours of credit (applicable to their programme) from September 1 of the preceding year to the following August 31. All other matters pertaining to eligibility I assumed to be the responsibility of the Athletic Director. These included matters such as amateur status, number of years of eligibility already consumed by each athlete; and eligibility pertaining to the transfer rule, including out-of-country training.

While this may sound simple, and straightforward, it often is not, given the human element which intrudes with all its weaknesses and personality quirks. I have often claimed that the competitiveness of the athletic arena carried over into this matter so that the desire, even need, to win is paramount. While I would never want a coach working for me that did not have this as a priority, surely this should not be at all costs. While I hope all would agree, throughout the years in which I have been involved in the athletic scene, I have seen (and heard so many rumours) of this almost desperateness in so many of the high-profile sports and by so many individuals in so many institutions and conferences that it is difficult not to have a somewhat jaded and cynical attitude. A few reasons for this all-too-pervasive attitude on the part of the coaches underscore some of the problems encountered by registrars.

The first is what I would term "wishful thinking", i.e., coaches and, even on occasion, athletic directors interpreting the regulations as they _think_ they are or indeed should be in the eyes of the beholder. Nowhere is this more prevalent as in the definition of what constitutes a professional league; a "practice" session, or even an exhibition game.

The second is what I refer to as the "no one will ever know" syndrome. This would apply to those student athletes whose secondary and even perhaps post-secondary education was obtained outside Canada, not only in the United States, but also Africa or Britain. For example, is a British soccer player who played with a university club (as opposed to the official university team) in an official league against other university club teams, eligible to participate in a C.I.A.U. sport immediately upon transfer?

The third, amazing reason, is total ignorance of the existence of an eligibility regulation, especially one which is sports-specific. There is a variant of this which involves a failure to comprehend the real meaning of the regulation.

A fourth problem encountered which is a bane of all of our operations is poor communications. Given the diversity of amateur sport organizations in Canada, and in many instances, the lack of clear-cut communication linkages between them, problems can and indeed do arise. For example, the C.I.A.U. has agreed to honour suspensions meted out by other national and provincial sport organizations. The problem is to determine who has been suspended for one year, for example, by the Ontario Soccer Association? Surely the coaches should know, but how do you expect an Athletic Director with perhaps 40 sports to be knowledgeable in such details, let alone a Registrar who may have no knowledge whatsoever about a particular sport and its organizational structure in his/her province or nationally?

I have reserved to the last, the people most directly involved, namely, the varsity athletes themselves. They are each required to sign the eligibility form but do they really understand to what their signature attests? Sadly, in many instances, I suspect not. In part, this emanates from the almost blind trust they have in their coaches and athletic director; in part, because they may never have been provided, not only with the actual C.I.A.U.

regulations, but also with the opportunity to raise questions of individuals knowledgeable in these guidelines. This problem area is certainly not unique to athletics. Indeed anyone who has served on disciplinary/appeal committees at an institution, knows the ease with which students affix their signatures to applications for admission, for residence, for course changes, etc. without ever reading them, or the regulations governing them.

Is there any effective way to overcome this major problem area which, as I have indicated, occurs in nonathletic areas as well? One approach has been to have a forum at which each potential varsity athletes is present and at which the conference and C.I.A.U. regulations are distributed, read, discussed and questions raised and hopefully answered. Athletic history forms are then signed in 3 places in front of a witness -- acknowledging receiving the regulations; reading them, and understanding them; and having been afforded the opportunity to raise questions with knowledgeable and responsible people. A penalty for falsification is clearly delineated. However, no procedure is foolproof and the bottom line still remains personal integrity.

Administrative Standards

In the preceding paragraphs, I have endeavoured to indicate that there are not standard procedures for determining the eligibility of students for varsity competition; each institutional system is undoubtedly different with a number of checks and balances within it. However, regardless of the system utilized, a Registrar has to be genuinely concerned in affixing his/her signature to an eligibility form because many of the documents required for a complete verification of the data are not available. Nor is the expertise to investigate some areas thoroughly.

Ethical Responsibility

Codes of ethics (for athletes, coaches and administrators) are integral portions of any athletic organization's by-law yet, in the particular case of eligibility, how do you legislate honesty? Is it enough merely to have stringent punitive measures upon discovery of falsification? By exposing the wrong-doers?

As a lead-in to the educational process vis-a-vis athletes, the C.I.A.U. has published a brochure for high school students. Copies of this are available. Yet I am always amazed at the "interpretations" of the rules by the parents of potential varsity athletes and even the athletes themselves. Furthermore, it is usually not difficult to determine who has assisted with this interpretation.

I have indicated previously how at least one institution is dealing with the continuing education of varsity athletes once they have enrolled in a member institution. However, a vital question arises as to whose responsibility it is "to blow the whistle". This is one of the most troublesome areas with which for four years as President of the C.I.A.U. I had to deal. Rumors arise about the amount of cheating allegedly going on at member institutions. Yet when these critics were challenged for detailed information, little if anything was forthcoming. When it was, it was duly checked and if violations were uncovered disciplinary measures ensued. As a Registrar, I wonder if I hear conflicting signals being issued - be truthful but do not become involved with the policing mechanism. Perhaps this was the dilemma which forced our colleagues to the south in the N.C.A.A. to employ at least 13 commissioners to investigate alleged infractions and why at least one of these commissioners has recently been hired by a member institution.

Other Matters Related to Eligibility

Five other aspects of eligibility and the current system also provide challenges for registrars.

First, whose responsibility is it to maintain a constant check to ensure that a varsity athlete continues to remain eligible throughout the playing season? If competing athletes alter their course load, they could become part-time and, hence, ineligible. Alternatively, who monitors whether they have become ineligible by virtue of playing for an outside team in the same sport in which they represent their institution?

Second, from a legal point of view, who actually has a right to the athletes/ grades at the end of term or academic year? Many institutions' Academic Calendar clearly indicate that information will not be released to a third party without the prior written consent of the student. Does this include coaches and athletic directors?

Third, what position should the registrar take when the "spirit" of the C.I.A.U. regulation is violated, although not technically the letter of the law? This is a situation which can arise relatively easily when students have been issued Letters of Permission to enrol in a course(s) at another institution with the expectation of transferring the credit hours earned back to the home institution. Usually there is a minimum grade necessary to effect this transfer. What happens to the requirement for athletic eligibility?

Fourth, do Registrars have the responsibility or should they expend the energy and time to "run down" leads on alleged eligibility problems? If so, who incurs the cost which can be considerable at times?

Fifth, what is the legality of a signature from an athlete who is a minor? This is a real question, given the age of some of the first and even second year varsity athletes at C.I.A.U. member institutions.

Items for Further Thought

Given the potential dangers of irregularities with varsity athletes' eligibility (whether deliberate or accidental), what would the President of a C.I.A.U. member institution do if his/her registrar refused to authorize an eligibility form -- not because of a known problem, but because of the potential pitfalls as noted earlier in this paper? Or, for that matter, what would the regional conference officers or the C.I.A.U. do? Personally I have never designated the responsibility of signing an athletic eligibility form to my associate registrar. This is not because I do not trust him, but because of the potential for major difficulties. These can arise with athlete eligibility forms more so than with any other forms which I am called upon to authorize.

What protection is afforded to a Registrar who authorizes a form in good faith only to have irregularities uncovered at a later date - irregularities which could not have been detected with the documentation available in the student's official University file?

Do Canadian universities really need athletic eligibility rules, or at least as many as currently exist? If so, are the existing ones too complex for easy understanding by the chief users -- students, coaches, A.D.'s, and other administrators? Those who have been around C.I.A.U. for as long as I have, can take the present rules and go down the pages, indicate particular problem people or areas which the rules were designed to redress. Nowhere is this more true than for men's basketball.

Conclusion

In drawing attention to some of the major concerns which I, as a registrar, have with existing eligibility, administrative and ethical matters, I hope to convince you, the chief executive officers of our C.I.A.U. member institutions that varsity athletes' eligibility and the official confirmation of this is a very serious matter, especially in these days of "legaleeze"; that the verification of this status is a collective responsibility of several university personnel; that these individuals are striving to fulfill their mandate in a very tricky area; that you need to become even more aware and develop an even deeper understanding of this explosive area, especially as you opt to become more directly involved in interuniversity athletics; that you ensure that, on your own campus, due procedures are in place and consistently followed by those directly responsible for varsity athletics; and, that you afford support (both legal and moral) to those who are charged with the responsibility of providing verification of athletic eligibility to organizations outside the institution. Since student-athletes are some of the greatest ambassadors for Canada's post-secondary educational system, I would trust that you would endeavour to work even more closely with athletic organizations, both regional and national, to address the problems and pitfalls inherent in eligibility matters. It is my opinion that the foundations are already in place but some of the bricks and mortar still require testing and perhaps even some repositioning.

Success can only be achieved by a deeper understanding and appreciation as well as more effective communications between the several partners in interuniversity athletics.

TOWARD EQUIVALENCE OF OPPORTUNITY

MARILYN POMFRET

The history and tradition of Canadian women's interuniversity athletic programs on a national base is comparatively short; just sixteen years have elapsed since the first National Championship was staged. Eastern Canada records a slightly longer competitive history for university women, but just 29 years ago the first university women's tournament champion was declared in Western Canada. Women's athletic programs have played and still play a frustrating game of catch-up.

Perhaps then, we should attribute the particular problems for university women athletes and their programs to youth; to growing pains. But wait. Are not the universities of Canada at the forefront of society's endeavours to improve and widen the spectrum of opportunities readily available for choice by women? The CAUT Council, by adoption of the 1985 'Statement on Positive Action to Improve the Status of Women in Canadian Universities' (Attridge, 1985) surely implied that to now, the answer has been No. Within sectors of the university then, perhaps within Athletic Departments, we may find the vision and leadership which will propel women toward equivalent stature? Again, a No and it is resounding.

I put to you first, that the primary problem faced by university women athletes, coaches, and administrators is that male chauvinism is alive and well in the minds and hearts of male athletic administrators and of those to whom they report. And the system is overweight with male athletic administrators. Full time positions in CIAU member institutions in 1978/79 were held by 53 men and 19 women; in 1981/82, by 71 men and 20 women; in 1982/83, by 79 men and 23 women (Vickers, 1984). Five years during the era of Universities' 'Equal Opportunity Employer' advertisements yielded four additional positions for women administrators and 26 new male faces.

Nonetheless, an optimistic thread can be found even here for athletic administrators, men and women, can be heard to say: 'Women's athletic programs are important for university women'. It is easy to say. The key now, however, is that women's programs must also be seen to be important; must be accorded the same development, energy, and recognition given to men's programs. Are they not, you may wonder and, once more, the answer is emphatically, No. The catch-up game is always played uphill; the chauvinistic attitude persists. Women's athletics may now be 'important' but men's athletic programs are somewhat more so. It shows in staffing and in budget allocations. It is apparent in insideous ways: The band which shows up at three-quarter time in the women's 'prelim' game, the athletic department's hype of the ice hockey game which does not extend to the field hockey game close by; the News Release wherein men's athletic achievements take up pages 1 and 2 while women's achievements may be found regularly on page 3; the athletic therapy room which is accessible only through the Men's Locker Room; the double-headers where Athletic Directors (women are generally Coordinators or Assist-ants) and University Presidents appear for the final three minutes of the women's game and stay throughout the men's event. The attitudes of those with responsibility for university athletics seeps through all levels of the unit, from the top to the staff to the athletes themselves and the system is thus perpetuated.

> "The last place where true equality will be realized is in an athletic setting. In an academic setting, students and professors would not tolerate a 3:00 - 5:00 pm laboratory time for male students, while women were assigned to the lab at dinner time." (West, 1984)

Can it really be accurate to assume that universities are not leading the sports world in the development of equivalence in opportunity for and percep-tion of the female athlete? From a vantage point of better than 20 years as a university athletic administrator and better than 20 years of close involve-ment with a Provincial sport governing body, I can assure you that Canadian universities are far and seriously at the rear of the pack. With apologies for a purely Western Canadian example, please note that on February 15, 1986 Lynne Williams became the 16th female 'Overall Athlete of the Year' during the 20th annual Sport British Columbia Awards Banquet. Less blatant examples of fair and equivalent programs abound throughout many Sport Governing bodies. Universities as well as the women's programs within, are definitely in the catch-up game in athletics.

Again, there are some optimistic threads to indicate that awareness is creeping in, albeit on quiet feet. For example, the scheduling for athletic facilities utilization clearly has become more equivalent. Men's and women's teams often practice side by side with encouragement and respect each for the other. The previously wide disparities in quality and quantity of equipment available have reduced. Nonetheless, I submit to you that it is beyond time for our Canadian universities to effect action which will ensure that sport programs for women are said to be important and equivalent, seen to be impor-tant in all aspects of their staging and, thereby, perceived to be equivalent to men's programs by the participants and the public alike. Here, as in all things, actions will speak louder than words.

As a first step toward that action, it serves well to review the volumes of men's and women's participation in the programs of the Canadian Interuni-versity Athletic Union (CIAU). First, we can agree, I believe, that current undergraduate enrollment in most of the 45 member institutions splits roughly 50% male and 50% female. With the addition of Cross Country (W) and Track & Field (M&W) in 1980/81, the CIAU program increased to 10 National Champion-ships for men and seven for women. The spread does not appear surprising on the surface, but beneath the surface lies the story. During 1982/83 on our campuses, there were 5079 males and 2159 females participating in the sport programs which lead to CIAU Championships; a ration of 2.4 to 1.0. The official 1985/86 figures have not yet been published but the trend analysis contained in the comparative study does not elicit hope for a ration improvement (Vickers and Gosling, 1984).

The study from which the 1982/83 participation figures have been taken became even more graphic when comparing the numbers of male and female participants in an 'equivalent category' of sports offered for men and women and for which the CIAU Regulations specify equal/similar roster sizes: basketball, cross country, women's field hockey/men's soccer, gymnastics, swimming & diving, volleyball. According to Vickers and Gosling "in each year, the number of male athletes in 'equivalent sports' exceeded that of women similarly categorized. In 1978, the difference amounted to 105 athletes but this discrepancy had increased to 357 male athletes by 1982" (p.10).

The questions have to be: Why is this so?; What factors are operative?; Are women students not turning out, not prepared to dedicate time and energy to pursuit of athletic excellence?

They turn out, they are dedicated, enthusiastic and determined, but too often, there is a lot of practice time for a very little competitive experience supported by a very little budget allocation. At The University of British Colombia, for example, they are in Badminton, Fencing and Tennis, in Rowing, Skiing, Soccer and Squash . . . but these are not in the CIAU or similarly organized interuniversity athletic programs.

People with world revered athletic reputations, John Landy (1986) for example, can see clearly that women athletes have earned a place:

> "Looking back to those days (1950-1960), when we now have
> examples of such superb middle distance runners as . . . ., it
> seems unbelievable that popular prejudice - seemingly backed
> by medical opinion - could have confined women to the
> sprints." (7)

We in women's athletics harbour the belief that our Universities have a responsibility to smooth the rough road to equivalence of opportunity for female athletes and thereby set an example for Canadian society. To this time, that responsibility has been met only to a token level but, sometimes rather grudgingly, we are keeping the faith and offering continuing chances for your positive future actions.

There must be leadership. Certainly, some men are competent to administer and/or coach women's sports and certainly, some men in Canadian university athletics speak with a forked-tongue, but these are not the role models so desperately needed at this time. Though the pool of candidates is smaller,

given the shorter time span of high performance competition for women, competent women who hold University degrees are available in both the administrative and coaching sectors. Their CV's may be shorter in the experience
category, but they have huge potential and they must have a chance to develop.
'Given equal credentials, we will hire the woman' is not a viable statement in
this instance, if ever the catch-up game is to be over.

Even the earlier figures cited for the comparative numbers of full-time
male and female athletic administrators in Canadian universities (1982/83: M =
79, W = 23) are highly misleading. Of the women listed, several are assigned
below 25% of workload for administration. Two or more have never seen the
entire University athletic budget. Some may be present at the CIAU Annual
General Meeting but not be voting delegates. Some are not present at all.
Presidents will have the opportunity to rectify the latter two situations when
asked to sign the CIAU form for University delegates to the 1986 AGM, June 8 -
15, 1986.

The Athletic Director is the primary architect of the attitudes evidenced
in all sectors of the sports program. From his leadership arise the nature of
the philosophy, ethics, and operating procedures which permeate the educational experience of each staff member and each athlete, male or female.

> "However, as in our patriarchal government, women often bring
> a unique perspective to issues. Therefore, when women are not
> elected and when women are selected or appointed in small
> numbers, the opportunity for different points of view is
> absent and dimensionality in formulating policy is diminished.
> Most governance systems in sports are patriarchal . . . "
> (West, 1984).

Need any more be said? Only that a considerably increased number of capable
and wise women administrators is vital to the formulation of future university
athletic policy.

The figures which indicate full-time coaching appointments for university
women's team, 1978/79 - 1982/83 and the trends which arise therefrom are
perhaps the most shocking of all. In that five year period, the number of
women head coaches of CIAU sports declined from 68 to 64 while, in the same
time period, the number of male head coaches of CIAU sports for women
increased from 22 to 47. (Vickers and Gosling, 1984).

> "The women were swept up by the optimism of the 1970's . . .
> The revolution seemed to have been won. . . This rather
> astonishing innocence quickly dissipated." (Berkinow, 1984).

Reality for women in several occupational areas, e.g., banking, law, architec-
ture, (and athletics), accompanied the discovery that "the road looks open but
is actually closed", (Berkinow, 1984), a condition which has become more
apparent in the economically strained 1980's and surely is a condition in the

CIAU. It is more than apparent that the head coaching position of a university women's team is an acceptable and sought after male role. The volume of male applications read by any search committee of recent years attests to this. But again, women coaches as well as women administrators must be visible and inspirational role models for the young if ever a balance is to be achieved.

For too long the sports world has been considered as the singular domain of the male -- the showcase for his virility and superior skills, a superiority somehow thought to reflect in all avenues of his life. In amateur sport, that era has gone. Man now shares his pedestal with outstanding female athletes and the participation base from which those who excel arise must be a foundation of equivalence of opportunity for the sexes.

Our Canadian interuniversity athletic programs do not now reflect that equivalent foundation. There are women, and some men as well, in university athletic administration who believe that the route to progress for women's programs is a return to the pre 1978 separate governance structure. Others, including myself, do not subscribe to this thinking. For me, the only way to improve a condition cannot be through segregation. To alter a cultural attitude one must surely be an integral part of that culture; it cannot be done in isolation. Rather, I prefer to believe that indeed, university women will catch-up and to place my occasionally shaky faith in the enlightened leadership and wisdom of Presidents and their administrations. Time will heal all only when their actions reflect understanding of the need to move rather swiftly to equivalence of opportunity!

Regardless of the program's confinement of my topic to problems unique to the female athlete, there is another kind of problem which I believe impacts heavily upon our universities and upon their men's and women's athletic programs and which I wish to take the liberty to address. I refer to the growing trend to legally separate if not divorce athletic departments from any academic unit within the university. In several instances, athletic departments appear to have become independent of the educational context in which they once existed. Certainly there is a chain for reporting, an accountability which too often is of a financial nature only; the bottom line. The philosophy and the policy, the values and the integrity, appear more and more to me to be deprived of accountability and attention related to the educational mission of the university. This trend leads us sadly to a little America model.

The pressures and the responses to them, which exist in the NCAA are apparent in the mini-form in the CIAU. In my view, it has become increasingly 'important', vital perhaps, to be ranked in the weekly Top Ten, to qualify for the Nationals. Recruitment 'strategies' and costs have altered to reflect this need and I detect that there is greater interest in athletic than in academic prowess. Fortunately, the CIAU has initiated an Academic Progress regulation. However, I suggest that the next study initiated should be of graduation rates, particularly among athletes in the high visibility, revenue producing sports.

Coaching appointments, I believe, tend recently and in greater numbers toward the short-term contract type on the premise that we don't want to get stuck with a non-producer. Produce here has to be read as the win-loss record and the coach must stack up the wins rather quickly to be assured of contract renewal. Further, we are all aware of recent scheduling of interuniversity and other competitions which take the student off the campus for more classroom days than in previous years.

Given that 'student' is the primary word in our CIAU By-laws phrase 'student-athlete', it would seem that the emphasis clearly must remain upon the elite educational experience with the additional opportunity to become an elite athlete.

There is hope that the educational context can remain the guideline for Canadian interuniversity athletics, for we are not too far along the proverbial road that is paved with good intentions. But there is some reeling in to be done I think, and it must start in the Presidents' offices with a review of philosophy, policy, integrity, and funding. In consultation with athletic and academic officials, the mutually agreed upon positions must pervade all athletic programs with accountability on all avenues as an absolute expectation.

Our student-athletes have many wonderful and valuable opportunities available to them. Not any one of us present today can afford the luxury of being a spectator to a diminishment of the quality of their experiences.

References

Attridge, Carolyn. CAUT Bulletin. Vol. 13, No. 1, p. 17, 1985.

Bernikow, Louise. We're Dancing As Fast As We Can. Savvy, April, 1984.

Landy, John. Canberra, Australia, Special to the Vancouver Sun, Jan. 23, 1986.

Vickers, Joan N. and Gosling, Barbara J. The Changing Participation of Men and Women in the Canadian Interuniversity Athletic Union (1978-1982). The Women's Representative Committee, CIAU. September, 1984, p. 23.

West, Charlotte. The Female Athlete - Who Will Direct Her Destiny. Rethinking Services for College Athletics. Schriberg & Brodzinski, F.R., December, 1984.

SECTION 5. INTERUNIVERSITY ATHLETICS: FUNDING THE PROGRAM

- WHO PAYS THE SHOT? -- H. JANZEN

- FUNDING INTERUNIVERSITY ATHLETICS IN CANADA: A STUDENT'S
  PERSPECTIVE -- L.E. MOHR

- DISCUSSION -- J. DICKINSON

WHO PAYS THE SHOT?

H. JANZEN

Most Canadian universities are experiencing severe financial restraints as the annual increases in income have been below what is required to maintain the existing operations. The results have been staffing and program cutbacks, coupled with the inability to upgrade existing programs and/or implement new programs.

The financial constraints have affected both athletic and academic programs. Today, at the same time as many universities are reducing their budgets, costs are escalating, particularly in travel and equipment. In addition, increased travel costs affect the Western Canada and Atlantic Canada regions more than Central Canada due to greater distances between the universities. Athletic directors are finding it increasingly difficult to operate their programs.

The responsibility for funding University athletic programs was reviewed 12 years ago. Matthews (1974), in his report "Athletics in Canadian Universities", found a great deal of variation in who was responsible for the funding of athletic programs.

Matthews reported that, in some universities, salaries and maintenance costs were a university responsibility while other operation costs were covered by an athletic fee. In some universities, the total cost of the intramural and recreational programs were seen as a more logical charge against university general funds then were intercollegiate sports. This lack of consistency in the funding of athletic programs illustrates what may have been an evolutionary process, largely dependent on the exigencies that existed on each individual campus over a period of years. Matthews recommended:

> "that the financial responsibility for the physical
> education and/or athletic and recreational programs
> be assumed by the institutions." (p.33)

Matthews warned administrators of the consequences of initiating institutional financing of athletic programs. He noted that the program must then be able to endure the rigors of academic scrutiny when justifying its budget requests and, further, that its budget would also be susceptible to the budgetary instability of fluctuating educational spendings.

Is it realistic, though, to expect athletic programs to be compared to academic programs when justifying budget requests? Is it not realistic to assume that, in times of fiscal restraint in an academic institution, academic programs would justifiably be placed at a higher priority than non-academic programs? Well, what has happened since 1974? Have there been dramatic changes in the financing of university athletic programs? Who is paying the shot today?

Survey

In an attempt to find answers to these questions, athletic directors from all of Canada's universities were contacted. Information regarding student athletic fees, gate receipts, corporate sponsorship, alumni support, operating grants from universities, and self-help programs illustrated the variety of ways that universities fund athletic programs.

For descriptive purposes the universities were grouped into four regions: Western Canada (N = 11 institutions), Ontario (N =16 institutions), Quebec (N = 4 institutions) and Atlantic Canada (N = 7 institutions). The following is a summary of these findings:

Compulsory Athletic Fees. With one exception, all universities in Western Canada have an athletic fee. Excluding the institution without a fee, the average is $25.00 and the range is from $10.00 to $43.50. The one institution that does not have a compulsory fee has a voluntary fee.

All but 2 of the universities in Ontario have an athletic fee. Of those with fees, the average is $36.00 and the range is $20.00 to $83.00. Five institutions' fees are over $50.00.

All universities in Quebec have a compulsory fee, the average being $58.00 and the range being $30.00 to $114.00.

In Atlantic Canada, 6 institutions do not have a fee while 4 have a compulsory fee. The average fee of the four is $33.00, the range $27.50 to $40.00.

Gate Receipts. There is some revenue generated from gate receipts, but it does not contribute significantly to the budget of most athletic programs. In the 11 universities in Western Canada, gate receipts range from $10,000 to $60,000. Seven institutions' gate receipts total less than $15,000. In Ontario universities, gate receipts range from $2,000 to $84,000. Eight universities receive less than $15,000 from the gate. Quebec and Atlantic Canada have 2 universities with no gate receipts. In the other institutions, the highest gate is $15,000, but most are between $5,000 and $10,000.

Alumni Support. Although support from Alumni Associations is extremely varied across the country, in general it does not have a significant impact on athletic budgets. Four universities in Western Canada receive no financial assistance from their Alumni Association, 3 receive approximately $10,000, and 4 receive $40,000, $50,000, $80,000 and $100,000. Seven schools in Ontario receive assistance from their Alumni Associations. While 4 receive less than $10,000, 1 institution receives $150,000. The largest amount that a school in Atlantic Canada receives from its Alumni Association is $30,000.

Sponsorship. Breweries, soft drink companies, shoe companies, and restaurants are typical kinds of corporate sponsors for athletic programs. Four institutions in Western Canada receive over $50,000. One school in each of Ontario and Quebec receives over $100,000, while the remaining institutions in Canada receive approximately $5,000 to $10,000.

Athletic Awards. Athletic awards, that is, monies awarded to students on the basis of athletic ability, are given only in Western Canada (Saskatchewan excluded). The reference in this report is to awards given by institutions and does not include awards, scholarships, etc. made by a third party (Alumni groups, etc.).

It is only in the last few years that athletic ability has been used as a criterion for loans, bursaries, scholarships, or other forms of awards offered by a university. The Matthews report recommended that athletic ability should not be a basis for awards.

Now, with the support of provincial governments, over $1.3 M is granted annually for athletic awards in Western Canada. Six institutions have an awards program that totals over $100,000 and 3 are over $200,000. Universities in Manitoba receive a total of $100,000 from the province on the basis that they provide a matching amount. Ontario institutions do not allocate any funds for this type of award. In Quebec, 5 schools do not allocate any funds for awards while 2 schools allocate $3,600 and $78,000 for such a program. The institutions in Atlantic Canada offer a total of $100,000 for awards. Four universities offer no awards program while 6 others allocate from $5,000 to $40,000.

Sport Camps. Many universities offer summer sport camps for non-university students. These camps not only generate income, but also familiarize students with the athletic and/or physical education programs. Sports camps are primarily found in Western Canada. Gross revenue, in one instance, is over $650,000 and in 3 others is over $250,000.

In Ontario, Quebec, and Atlantic Canada, the majority of institutions do not receive significant income from sport camps. There are, however, 3 institutions in Ontario that receive $200,000, $100,000 and $50,000 respectively, while in Quebec and Atlantic Canada, there is one institution in each association that receives $180,000 plus.

Operation & Maintenance Expenses. The responsibility for covering operation and maintenance costs (heat, energy, caretaking services) for recreational/athletic facilities varies considerably throughout Canada. In the West, 3 of 11 athletic departments are required to provide some support (less than $200,000.) for these expenses. In Ontario, 2 institutions' athletic departments cover 100% of operation and maintenance costs, one institution covers $100,000, while in the remaining 13 institutions these costs are covered by the general operating budget of the university. In the majority of institutions in Quebec and Atlantic Canada, these costs are covered by the general operating budget of the university.

Summary

It may not be realistic to expect athletic programs to be completely funded by central funds from the universities, but it is evident that there are a variety of self-help sources of income to provide revenue for athletic departments. Gate receipts, facility rental, athletic fees, locker fees, towel and equipment rentals, sport club and non-credit course registration fees, corporate sponsorship, alumni support, and sport camps all play a very significant role in the make-up of many athletic budgets throughout Canada.

In the past years of financial restraint, it has been primarily through the innovative and careful planning of athletic directors that the athletic programs in Canada have been maintained. It is only through further creativity in developing self-help income activities that athletics will continue to develop and expand. If athletic directors rely only on university operating grants and/or athletic fees to finance their programs, we will see, in the near future, the withering and dying of athletic programs.

The major challenge for athletic departments is to generate income without losing control over their programs and without compromising the educational philosophy inherent in them.

Reference

Matthews, A.W., "Athletics in Canadian Universities", Association of Universities and Colleges of Canada, Ottawa, 1974.

FUNDING INTERUNIVERSITY ATHLETICS IN CANADA:
A STUDENT'S PERSPECTIVE

LARRY E. MOHR

Athletics has always been an integral part of virtually every student's university life. As the number of students in Canadian universities has increased, so has the size of the athletic programs that have to be administered and funded. This growth in size and scope of programs offered by Canadian universities has predictably put strains on the people and organizational structures set up to administer them.

New personnel and new administrative structures are sometimes called for as a solution to these problems. New attitudes toward sport and a commitment to get out and "sell" the program lead many to advocate a reorientation of the athletic programs in Canadian universities. New marketing techniques are advocated as methods of promoting the university and increasing revenues to the university. Creation of national training centres and a cadre of high profile, well funded coaches and athletes are put forward as the way to generate community and media interest in Canadian interuniversity athletics. Removing athletics from the administration of Physical and Health Education departments is often seen as the first step toward creating a more positive and professional attitude toward interuniversity athletics in Canada.

It seems that almost everyone can give an opinion about what is wrong with athletics in Canadian universities. Very few though will give you any concrete suggestions as to how these problems are to be overcome. Any scheme designed to solve the problems of interuniversity athletics must start with a consideration of where the money is to be found to finance the program. I would say that on the whole too much time is spent creating plans and not enough time is spent making them operational. Making them operational means finding the money to make them go. More often than not financing is an afterthought to the planning process, an error which dooms many well-intentioned plans to failure.

I would argue that financing considerations must be part of the entire strategic planning process for interuniversity athletics in Canadian universities. The issue of who should pay for the interuniversity athletic program cannot be separated a priori from the determination of what type of program will be funded. The following is a discussion of the alternative sources of funding for interuniversity athletics, and a discussion of the implications of strategic choices for the funding decision.

The student's perspective is taken, arguing that the student fees should only be used to finance those aspects of the interuniversity athletic program from which the student body derives some direct benefits. I speak only for myself and not for Queen's University.

Role of Interuniversity Athletics in Canadian Universities

As university budgets tighten and interuniversity athletic budgets grow, more and more administrators are looking seriously at alternative ways of organizing the interuniversity athletic program within their universities. Many universities have reached a crossroads in the development of their programs. Many are likely to reach the conclusion that the existing administrative and financial structures will not be adequate in the future if existing athletic programs are to be maintained and expanded.

There is the potential for a major strategic shift in the thinking of university administrations regarding what they expect from the athletic program and what resources the university is prepared to invest in these programs. Tightening university budgets means that there will be more and more pressure on athletics to "pay its own way". It is foolish to believe that universities will be content to continue to invest money in the athletics program and not monitor the results in some way.

It is in this way that the financial considerations will ultimately impact the future of interuniversity athletics in Canadian universities. Tight budgets at all levels of the university will mean that, more and more, financial considerations will enter the decision as to what programs to support. This must raise concern on the part of athletic administrators now facing the prospect of having their programs evaluated by university officials intent on saving money.

The Strategic Choices

There is a fundamental choice to be made regarding two broad directions that Canadian interuniversity athletics could pursue. These two general direction answer implicitly the question of what the role of interuniversity athletics should be in Canadian universities. I make generalizations that undoubtedly overstate these respective positions, but only the general philosophy of the positions is important here. The extreme portrayals only serve to facilitate discussion of the two positions.

The first alternative is to support a program whose goal is to provide the opportunity for as many students as possible to experience interuniversity competition. There would be less emphasis on producing winning teams and producing world class athletes. Participation and education are the priorities in such a system. I will refer to the above system as the "Participative Model".

The second alternative would see interuniversity athletics as a vehicle for gaining national recognition for individuals, teams, and universities. The emphasis in the interuniversity athletics program would be on producing national champions, and world class athletes and coaches. I will refer to the above system as the "Elite Model".

Ontario universities have so far remained committed in general to the first alternative. The Rickerd Report (1985) reaffirmed the conviction of Ontario universities to the principle that participation in athletics is an integral part of the student's education, "Ontario universities desire to give their students genuine opportunities to participate in interuniversity athletics."(p.21) The mission of the interuniversity athletics program is to provide all students with an opportunity to experience competition. This can only be accomplished through a strictly amateur system. Scholarships for athletes are rejected on the grounds that scholarships would be inconsistent with the notion that universities are first and foremost an educational institution. Paying athletes to play is contrary to the principles of such a system.

Sources Of Financing

Student Fees. As Table 1 illustrates, there is a wide variation of what students pay for athletics in Ontario universities. One cannot push these numbers too far as each university differs as to what the student fees cover. Even so, we get a broad picture of how differently students at various universities within one province are treated. Carleton University charged the highest student fees ($77 per student) in 1983-84 while offering one of the lowest number of sports (13) at the interuniversity level. On the other side, Queen's University charged one of the lowest fees ($30 per student) while offering the largest number of interuniversity sports (41).

Clearly there is much inequity in the system with regard to student contributions to athletics. Much of this inequity arises because student fees cover different aspects of the program at different universities. This highlights the point that it is not at all clear as to what portion of the costs students should be required to pay for.

Table 1 also highlights the point that students at various universities are not provided with the same opportunities to participate in interuniversity competition, as the variance in the number of sports offered by universities is striking. This variance cannot be explained away by the differences in the student fees collected. There is a large amount of variance even between universities of comparable size and student fees. For example, Ottawa University and McMaster University each have close to 12,000 students and have student fees of $35 and $32 respectively. Ottawa U. offers 7 interuniversity sports while McMaster offers 37. How can these differences by explained?

I would argue that the process of rationalizing interuniversity athletics has already begun at many universities. Even in Ontario there is a great deal of variance over what Ontario universities consider to be a commitment to a "broad" interuniversity athletics program. The idea of maintaining athletics for the students is a romantic idea, but it is clear that not every university is prepared to pay for the romance.

General University Funds. As the other major source of funds to the interuniversity program, university funds also must vary widely across Ontario and Canada. I come to this conclusion even through there are no public data available on how much is spent at the various institutions. The variation in student fees at various universities suggests that the amount of funds that the universities pay is also widely variable. Everyone is aware of the budget cuts imposed on universities in virtually every province, forcing administrators to take a long hard look at their commitment to various academic and athletic programs. As athletic programs are evaluated in comparison to academic programs in the competition for university funds, administrators must compare the value of maintaining a broad interuniversity athletics program with the value of maintaining academic programs. It is in this environment that supporters of the Participative Model of athletics have difficulty in convincing administrators that the university gains some benefit from maintaining sports that have little potential for generating revenues and/or interest in the university itself.

Proponents of the Elite Model can counter that investing in a program that supports high profile sports has the potential to generate considerable benefits to the university as a whole. How much is three hours worth of prime time on one of the major networks to the two universities who make it to the Vanier Cup or to the CIAU finals in basketball or hockey? The publicity, goodwill, and the alumni dollars that such an appearance can generate are tangible benefits that university officials can see on the bottom line. I think that it is inevitable that university administrations will begin insisting that athletics begin to pay more of its own way within the university community.

Alumni. I do believe that alumni constitute an underutilized source of money to interuniversity athletics. The ability of universities to tap into this source, however, is uneven as the older universities simply have more alumni upon which to draw. Rules exist which restrict institutions from generating additional revenue from corporate sponsors and alumni. I doubt whether there is much potential for this source of funds to be of much assistance in the short run.

Government. The federal government has often toyed with the idea of creating a series of national training centres across Canada as homes for national teams. Assuming that this would generate revenues to the universities directly, this could serve as an alternate source of funding.

I believe that this development is not consistent with the Participative Model of interuniversity athletics. The emphasis in a training centre is to produce world class competitors; the goal is to attract better athletes, not necessarily better students. Any funding of such a concept should be kept entirely separate from the regular interuniversity program, as it limits the opportunities for students to participate. Student fees should not be used to fund such an initiative, as the student body derives few benefits from such a training centre. National training centres are an idea forwarded by the federal government because it hopes to achieve national priorities. Students generally should not be asked to pay for any part of such a program; if the federal government feels that the national benefits received from operation of a national training centre justify the costs, then the government itself should pay the entire cost of running the centre.

I also have serious reservations about what the impact of such a move would be on the existing league structures. We already see serious imbalances in the level of competition as the schools which have become training centres for national team athletes dominate interuniversity competition. Does it really make sense for regular students from across Canada to try to compete with national team athletes who have the benefits of superior coaching and the use of better facilities for training? National team training centres render interuniversity competition meaningless, as regular student athletes cannot compete with these competitors on an equal basis. I cannot see the point of a university remaining in the interuniversity league structure if its team is the same or similar to the national team.

The Minister of Amateur Sport, the Honourable Otto Jelinek, has also indicated that the federal government would like to reduce its financial commitment to amateur athletics. He said on January 21, 1986, "As amateur sports grow, the monetary resources have to increase as well and there's only so much you can achieve from the taxpayer. It would be irresponsible to dip further into the public purse." (Globe and Mail, January 22, 1986) He said this while announcing the creation of a marketing agency for amateur athletics, designed to attract corporate sponsors and their money to amateur athletics. Government revenues will not be forthcoming to solve the problems of Canadian interuniversity athletics.

Media Revenues. Advertising dollars and marketing revenues are always looked upon as the great panacea to all of the financing problems of Canadian interuniversity athletics. No doubt that the big television revenues garnered by some of the big schools in the U.S. initiate this view. I am somewhat skeptical of the potential of this source for Canadian universities.

Even if we were to accept the Elite Model across the country, I doubt seriously if media revenues would increase appreciably. To increase this source of revenues, universities would have to market their athletes much more vigorously than is done currently. Even in the high profile sports of football, hockey, and basketball putting the CIAU championship game on national television does not generate great interest on the part of the Canadian public. Not having heard of or seen these teams play all season, it is foolish to expect Canadians to flock to the Vanier Cup or other national championships. Without this interest, the ability of the CIAU to acquire significantly more media revenues is limited. This interest can only be created through an ongoing program of promotion of each university on a national level. This is beyond the capabilities of most universities at the present time.

Financing the Future

We return again to the question of who should pay for the interuniversity athletics program in Canadian universities. It has been argued here that it is unlikely that alumni and media revenues can be looked to in the short run as major sources of revenues for athletic directors. I would similarly be skeptical of the national training centre concept as a solution to the general funding problem. This leaves us then with the choice of increasing student fees or increasing the portion paid by the university.

One of my main assertions has been that the financing decisions must be made in parallel with the strategic choices facing athletics administrators generally. The choice of the model of development will go a long way to determining the sources of funding that must be looked to.

The department of economics teaches that the only just and efficient way of allocating responsibility for financing services to individuals is to make the individuals or groups who receive the benefits of the service pay for it. In this way the right amount of the goods or services will be offered to the public as those who derive the benefits from an activity determine the value of those benefits. In the same way, one can argue that the responsibility for funding interuniversity athletics should fall to those who expect to benefit from the program.

If one was to accept the Participative Model of development, which emphasizes participation by the student body, one must automatically look to the student fees as the primary source of funding for the program.

Students would be able to decide how much the services they receive from the program are worth, and accordingly would refuse to pay more than that amount in student athletic fees. In this way the interuniversity athletics program would be the optimum size.

If one accepts the Elite Model of development, emphasizing high performance, one must look primarily to the university as the main source of revenue. The objective of the program is to develop athletes and coaches that potentially can bring publicity or recognition to the university. This being the case, the burden of funding the interuniversity program must fall to the university which can then decide how much value to place on these activities, and accordingly how much money to spend on them.

Neither scenario is entirely applicable as the interuniversity program is funded at most universities through some combination of these sources. But the implications of the models are clear. If universities choose to cling to a broadly based (i.e., many sports) interuniversity athletic program, athletic directors shall have to turn more and more to the student body for funding. Such a move will undoubtedly lead to increased student demands which will put pressure on athletic directors to broaden their programs still further.

If universities choose to concentrate their interuniversity effort and dollars on high profile sports, athletic directors will have to look more and more to general university funds to support the interuniversity athletics program. This will undoubtedly lead to a further narrowing of programs as pressures by university administrators on athletic directors increase to drop programs that cannot be justified financially.

One should also note here the impact that such a system could have on the equality of the sexes in Canadian university athletics. Male sports are generally able to garner more media attention than female sports, and, therefore, one might expect to see a diminution of the athletic opportunities open to females in the interuniversity athletics programs.

The net result is a polarization within Canadian universities as to the source of financing of their interuniversity athletic programs and the objectives of the program. I believe that students will be willing to pay increased student fees to support a broadly based interuniversity program in which all students have the opportunity to participate. I do not believe, however, that students will be content to sit idly by and see their money spend on an elite group of athletes and an interuniversity program that brings few benefits to the student body generally. If students are to be expected to pay an increasing share of the costs, then they will demand an increasing share of the power to determine how those monies are spent.

I see the interuniversity athletic system in Canada fragmenting along these two lines. The conflicts have surfaced several times over the past few years; first in the conflict between Ontario-Quebec and the Atlantic-Western Canada groups over the use of scholarships to athletes, and, secondly, in the recent Big Four proposal by four universities in Ontario and Quebec. Both of these conflicts reflect the deeper philosophical and strategic decisions that universities have made or are making. All of them return to the question of what the role of interuniversity athletics should be in Canadian universities. Undoubtedly, these same divisions will arise at this conference and future conferences.

I am not sure that this basic conflict can be resolved because strategic decisions cannot be reversed without tremendous cost. Within the Canadian university community, universities have made different choices which have led them down different roads. The choice now is whether to try and get everyone back on the same track or to accept these differences. If these differences cannot be overcome it is inevitable that realignment or tiering of some sort will be necessary as the two groups become more polarized.

Universities with narrow programs will have more resources to devote to fewer sports, allowing them to hire better coaches and provide better facilities and equipment for their teams. Universities with broad programs will see their limited resources spread over more and more sports, making it difficult for them to financially attract the coaches required for them to remain competitive. Facilities and equipment will also deteriorate, making it difficult for them to continue to attract better student-athletes. The result is a growing imbalance in the level of competition that each university can offer.

I would expect fellow students to demand to compete with universities and athletes that start at the same relative level. Interuniversity competition will have lost all value if, at the outset, certain universities' athletes have an overwhelming advantage over their competition. Competition will cease to be competition at all. One can expect to quickly lose student support for a program that cannot be competitive. Unless some semblance of equality of programs can be preserved, universities can expect to quickly lose the support of their student bodies for their interuniversity athletics program.

References

Council of Ontario Universities "Report of the Special Committee on Intercollegiate Athletics." The Rickerd Report, Toronto, 1985.

TABLE 1

(1984-85 figures)

	INSTITUTIONAL PARTICIPATION ** IN INTERUNIVERSITY ATHLETICS			STUDENT ATHLETIC	
	MENS	WOMENS	TOTAL	FEES ***	ENROLLMENT ***
	----	------	-----	--------	----------
BROCK	14	8	22	n.a.	n.a.
CARLETON	7	6	13	$77	10,000
GUELPH	18	13	31	40	11,000
LAURENTIAN	8	7	15	30	3,100
LAURIER	14	11	25	40	4,500
McMASTER	21	16	37	32	11,500
OTTAWA	5	4	9	35	12,500
QUEEN'S	22	19	41	30	11,000
RMC	14	4	18	n.a.	n.a.
RYERSON	7	7	14	n.a.	n.a.
TORONTO	22	19	41	n.a.	40,000
TRENT	10	3	13	63	2,800
WATERLOO	19	15	34	36	16,000
WESTERN	22	18	40	54	20,000
WINDSOR	13	9	22	10	8,000
YORK	17	13	30	n.a.	16,000

** - figures from the Special Committee on Intercollegiate
     Athletics - Council of Ontario Universities, 30 April, 1985

*** - figures are estimates

DISCUSSION ON "INTERUNIVERSITY ATHLETICS:
FUNDING THE PROGRAM"

J. DICKINSON, MODERATOR

Unidentified Speaker: Mr. Mohr, when you talked about students supporting programs, you suggested that if there were a narrow number of elite programs competing all over Canada, the students wouldn't support it. I take it, therefore, that you negated fan support being involved in the program. If that is the case, why would the students at your school support interuniversity athletics when only 5% of the student population gets to participate?

Mr. Larry Mohr: Well, I think that fan support is one reason that students continue to be willing to support the program. But they will only continue to support the program if they go to the games, and they won't go to the games if our teams consistently lose. They are not going to go if our team gets slaughtered every Saturday afternoon or every Friday night. Once that happens, you are going to get total apathy in the student body as to the value of the program. If there is no school spirit created, and that generally happens in winning teams, your program is not successful.

Same questionner: But you would support a school that had two teams that were outstanding and winning Canadian championships and the student body was going because they were winning. You think that school would survive on this?

Mr. Larry Mohr: No, that is not what I'm saying. I'm saying that the students have to believe that they are receiving some benefit from the program. I would say that fan support is probably just a marginal contribution to that. I would say that the more important reason that they continue to support the program is that the program is open to all students to participate on campus and that you can, as a regular student, have a real opportunity to make a team. Whether you choose to do that is your decision, but you have the opportunity. I think if we go to elite sports, where the level of competition is raised to such a level that normal students cannot compete, then they will not support that program.

Ms. Abby Hoffman: I want to repeat, in part, the point I made earlier about the York University competitive advantage in sport where this advantage is the result of a number of years of commitment to the sport including technical leadership and so on. It has nothing to do with the highly probable situation of that university getting a high performance centre in that sport. Having said that though, I think that many of the points that you made in your presentation are extremely valid. They pertain to or revolve around that whole issue of depending on what the objectives of your program are and the extent that you go after certain kinds of funding sources. I think that's very reasonable. The other point you made though, is that various institutions, partly because of the source of funds into which they can tap, and for other reasons -- size, location, whatever -- have tremendously varying philosophies, tremendously varying resources. But the logical conclusion of that is not to aspire to any sort of concensus that would allow competition in interuniversity sport to occur among all institutions. Rather I suggest we should be working towards a purity of competitive activity in interuniversity sport such that various factors, various characteristics of universities, be it their size, regional location, sources of funding, their philosophies, or whatever, would somewhere or other be rolled up as the determinant of a rational set of criteria for classification of the universities and sports into a peer competitive structure. Essentially what I am saying is that I don't understand the premise for some of the comments that you have made. Why has the subject of tyranny in intercollegiate athletics taken so long to be put on the table and in fact to be acted upon? I see this as a logical conclusion of the kind of information and approach that was put on the table today.

Mr. Larry Mohr: I agree with you. My perception is that we have two different philosophies, and every university has a different degree to which they support each philosophy. We have two competing philosophies and the question I raised at the beginning has apparently been reconciled and is "can we live with those philosophies"? I think every CIAU meeting tries to do that. The question we seriously have to ask ourselves is, is this possible? And if it is not possible, then maybe we should just accept that and move on. And if we have certain universities who want to pursue a different model then why should we hold them back? If some universities want to pursue a broad program and have 45 sports, then why can't they do that? And if some schools want to concentrate on 3 or 4 or 5 sports, then why can't they do that? Why do we have to try to bring them all under one umbrella and force one set of standards on them? Then we sit around the table and everyone throws recriminations back and forth as to which model is best. Maybe there is no end to this. Maybe they are both fine in their own milieu. Determining the sources of funding is just one aspect of that decision.

Dr. Stu Robbins: Perhaps, as it has come up twice, I ought to respond to the York gymnastics program. I would first say that it began as a conscious decision by the Department to stress gymnastics. From its outset, the Department took a survey of the school and asked what were the things which were being ignored in the university Physical Education program. And the answer came loud and clear -- gymnastics. Therefore, the program put a stress on gymnastics. I would like to say I'm embarrassed by the facility in which we practise at York. It is probably one of the worst in the country. The budget for gymnastics is between $2000 and $3000. The coach is an entrepreneur and we also run a very successful program for children which helps support the equipment, but the budget is very low.

Unidentified Speaker: Mr. Mohr, I would like to take umbrage with your point about tiering. I have been a proponent of tiering for some time and the real problem with tiering is that a lot of people feel that the bottom tier is too bad a tier to be in. They will not accept that level. I have no trouble with trying to climb from the 26th tier. But only as long as the competition is equitable.

Mr. Larry Mohr: Mr. Chairman, just to make another point, we have one team and 44 clubs at Queens, and this is the problem with tiering. It is compounded by the fact that we want to play in different tiers within the sport. We have a structure that makes that very hard to break down. We resist that kind of movement. I would suggest that the kind of move we have made in Ontario is trying to break that structure down and form a new league and then cross over, but that is one of our big problems.

Mr. Paul Wilson: I would just like to say one other thing - that I think is a strength in our profession. I am quite happy at Trent to offer a totally different program than any other university in Ontario. The student has a choice. He knows he has to pay whatever money he has to pay before he comes. And, he knows the programs we offer so I think that's fine.

Mr. Larry Mohr: My response to that would be, within a province don't you want to have some understanding of equality? If the universities are going to compete amongst each other, shouldn't all programs be given at least an equal chance for the resources, so that they're in the same ballpark at the beginning?

Dr. J. Dickinson: Our time is up and I would like to thank Dr. Janzen and Mr. Mohr and the questioners for the excellent presentations and discussion.

SECTION 6. SUMMARY

- FUTURE DIRECTIONS FOR CANADIAN INTERUNIVERSITY ATHLETICS:
  A SUMMARY OF THE CONFERENCE -- A.W. TAYLOR

FUTURE DIRECTIONS FOR CANADIAN INTERUNIVERSITY
ATHLETICS: A SUMMARY OF THE CONFERENCE

A.W. TAYLOR

The stimuli through the Canadian Council of University Physical Education Administrators (CCUPEA) for this conference were primarily three fold:

a.   the findings of the 1984-85 Council of Ontario Universities (COU) Committee investigating intercollegiate sport in the two Ontario leagues (Rickerd Report);

b.   the necessity to investigate the different roles played by university sport in the five conferences across this broad nation; and,

c.   the need to determine the relationship between interuniversity athletes, Physical Education, and the central administration of universities across Canada.

It is my intention to briefly refer to these purposes, and to try to put them into some perspective in conjunction with the program presented today.

I was fortunate enough to sit as a member of the COU Committee which investigated the role of interuniversity athletics within the Ontario University Athletic Association (OUAA) and Ontario Women's Intercollegiate Athlete Association (OWIAA). After interviews with most of the Chief Executive Officers (CEC) and other senior university administrative personnel, Executive members of the OUAA and the OWIAA, it became quite clear that many CEO's were poorly informed as to the role and daily administration of interuniversity athletics in Ontario. However, it became apparent that, because of the inordinate amount of media coverage of university sport and because of a proposed break away of three of the oldest and largest institutions in Ontario, that all was not well. As a result, a Commission to govern Ontario interuniversity athletics was formed and this group is currently in place. It is a most unfortunate reflection of the state of athletics in Ontario that external auditors had to be assigned to attempt to regulate and monitor irregularities in admission and academic progress of student athletes. I trust this is an attempt by the COU to generate continuing fair competition among university student/athletes and to prevent the development of an insidious system that would incorporate athlete/students. Believe me, the difference between these two types of individuals is more than subtle and these differences have been duly emphasized by Abby Hoffman, Roger Jackson, Mary Keyes, Darwin Semotiuk, Marilyn Pomfret, and Elizabeth Chard in their presentations.

It has become apparent today, primarily after hearing the papers of George Connell, Greg Mackinnon, Jean-Guy Ouellet, Henry Janzen, and Larry Mohr that the problems interuniversity athletics face are similar across Canada. However, the different areas of the country, the different conferences and the universities within these different areas have attempted different solutions to the problems. There does not appear to be an integrated attempt to resolve the problems in a unified manner. In all likelihood, such a resolution is not possible without some unified body offering leadership to resolve the issues at hand. Perhaps the CIAU could offer assistance in this instance. A starting point may be to offer to the CEO's and league administrators a copy of the recommendation of the COU committee (Rickerd Report 1985). The major recommendations are as follows:

1. that each university develop a statement of philosophy on interuniversity athletics, embodying certain defined principles, and have this statement formally approved by the Senate and Board of Governors;

2. that each university provide an administrative structure that functions in support of women's athletics;[1]

3. that each university accept minimum eligibility requirements for participation in interuniversity athletics that are acceptable throughout the conference.[2]

It should be hoped that if each university's CEO developed, in conjunction with the administrators of interuniversity athletes, these appropriate tenets and made certain they were judiciously applied, the majority of the problems would be at least partially alleviated.

Well, where are we going? What are our future directions? Don Macintosh and John Dewar have told us where we came from and where we have been. I would suggest to you that we are heading in a direction not dissimilar from that taken in the United States more than 50 years ago. Today, as is obvious from the situations at Georgia, TCU, Clemson, and Alabama, we must guarantee that the role of interuniversity athletics in Canada, does not follow the NCAA pathway to its present destination. We must guarantee an academic stability to athletics, an integrity based upon moral and ethical and academic standards. We must guarantee the existence of the student/athlete and prevent the rise of the athlete/student. It is my contention that one means to prevent this change in direction is to give interuniversity athletics an academic base. This can be accomplished most appropriately and most directly within the Canadian milieu by placing athletics under the administration of Physical Education. I leave you with this thought for consideration and direction.

---

1. See the paper by Marilyn Pomfret
2. See papers by Darwin Semotiuk, Mary Keyes, Elizabeth Chard

I would further suggest to you that interuniversity athletics in Canada are relatively healthy. We should continue in the direction we are going only if we maintain the concept of student/athlete. As Henry Janzen and Larry Mohr pointed out to us, finances are probably the greatest problem facing athletics in Canadian Universities today. If athletics are important to an institution, surely the onus lies within the universities and the conferences to develop fund raising schemes, with no strings attached, to support our athletic endeavours. In conclusion, I would suggest to you that Interuniversity Athletics need and deserve financial assistance, an academic base, a set of philosophical principles passed by the University Senate, and greater contact between the administrators in charge of the institutions and the administrators of athletic programs. We need continued dialogue, communication, and cooperation between the athletic conferences, the CIAU, Sport Canada, and the Canadian Olympic Association (COA) to guarantee opportunity for excellence in academics and athletics in Canadian institutions.

References

Council of Ontario Universities "Report of the Special Committee on Intercollegiate Athletics: The Rickerd Report" Toronto, April, 1985.